Daily Academic Vocabulary

Grade 3

Editorial Development: Bonnie Brook Communications
Content Editing: Marilyn Evans
Leslie Sorg
Copy Editing: Sonny Bennett
Art Direction: Cheryl Puckett
Cover Design: Cheryl Puckett
Illustration: Jim Palmer
Design/Production: Carolina Caird
Arynne Elfenbein

EMC 2759

Helping Children Learn since 1979

Congratulations on your purchase of some of the finest teaching materials in the world.

Photocopying the pages in this book is permitted for <u>single-classroom use only</u>. Making photocopies for additional classes or schools is prohibited.

Correlated to State Standards

Visit *teaching-standards.com* to view a correlation of this book's activities to your state's standards. This is a free service.

CPSIA: Printed by McNaughton & Gunn, Saline, MI USA. [8/2010] Book
CPSIA: Lehigh Phoenix, 8111 North 87th St., Milwaukee, WI USA. 53224 [8/2010] Transparencies

Contents

About Academic Vocabulary

What Is Academic Vocabulary?

Academic vocabulary is that critical vocabulary that students meet again and again in their reading and classroom work across all content areas. Feldman and Kinsella refer to these high-use, widely applicable words—words such as *compare*, *occurrence*, *structure*, *sequential*, *symbolize*, and *inference*—as "academic tool kit words."[1]

Why Is Academic Vocabulary Instruction Important?

Vocabulary knowledge is one of the most reliable predictors of academic success. Studies show a major difference over time between the achievement levels of children who enter school with a strong oral vocabulary and those who begin their schooling with a limited vocabulary. Dr. Anita Archer says, "In many ways the 'Reading Gap,' especially after second and third grade, is essentially a Vocabulary Gap—and the longer students are in school the wider the gap becomes."[2] Focused vocabulary instruction can reduce this gap.

Knowing academic vocabulary—the "vocabulary of learning"—is essential for students to understand concepts presented in school. Yet academic English is not typically part of students' natural language and must be taught. "One of the most crucial services that teachers can provide, particularly for students who do not come from academically advantaged backgrounds, is systematic instruction in important academic terms."[3]

What Does Research Say About Vocabulary Instruction?

Common practices for teaching vocabulary—looking up words in the dictionary, drawing meaning from context, and impromptu instruction—are important but cannot be depended upon alone to develop the language students need for academic success.

Most vocabulary experts recommend a comprehensive vocabulary development program with direct instruction of important words. *Daily Academic Vocabulary* utilizes direct teaching in which students use academic language in speaking, listening, reading, and writing. Used consistently, *Daily Academic Vocabulary* will help students acquire the robust vocabulary necessary for academic success.

[1]Feldman, K., and Kinsella, K. "Narrowing the Language Gap: The Case for Explicit Vocabulary Instruction." New York: Scholastic, 2004.
[2]Archer, A. "Vocabulary Development." Working paper, 2003. (http://www.fcoe.net/ela/pdf/Anita%20Archer031.pdf)
[3]Marzano, R. J. and Pickering, D. J. *Building Academic Vocabulary*. Alexandria, VA: Association for Supervision and Curriculum Development, 2005.

Tips for Successful Vocabulary Teaching

The "Weekly Walk-Through" on pages 6 and 7 presents a suggested instructional path for teaching the words in *Daily Academic Vocabulary*. Here are some ideas from vocabulary experts to ensure that students get the most from these daily lessons.*

Active Participation Techniques

- Active participation means ALL students are speaking and writing.
- Use **choral responses**:
    - Pronounce the word together.
    - Read the sentence/question together.
    - Complete cloze sentences together.
- Use **nonverbal responses**:
    - Students give thumbs-up signal, point to the word, etc.
    - Make sure students wait for your signal to respond.
- Use **partner responses**:
    - Have students practice with a partner first.
    - Listen in on several pairs.
- Allow thinking time before taking responses.
- Randomly call on students; don't ask for raised hands.
- Ask students to rephrase what a partner or other classmate said.

Model and Practice

- Use an oral cloze strategy when discussing a new word. Invite choral responses. For example: *If I read you the end of a story, I am reading you the _____.* (Students say, "conclusion.")
- Complete the open-ended sentence (activity 1 on Days 1–4) yourself before asking students to do so.
- Make a point of using the week's words in your conversation and instruction (both oral and written). Be sure to call students' attention to the words and confirm understanding in each new context.
- Encourage students to look for the week's words as they read content area texts.
- Find moments during the day (waiting in line, in between lessons) to give students additional opportunities to interact with the words. For example:

    *If what I say is an example of **accomplish**, say "accomplish." If what I say is <u>not</u> an example of **accomplish**, show me a thumbs-down sign.*

    > *I meant to clean my room, but I watched TV instead.* (thumbs down)
    > *Stacia read two books a week, more than any other student.* ("accomplish")
    > *The scientists found a cure for the disease.* ("accomplish")
    > *The mechanic could not fix our car.* (thumbs down)

---

* See also page 9 for specific ideas for English language learners.

Weekly Walk-Through

Each week of *Daily Academic Vocabulary* follows the same five-day format, making the content more accessible for both students and teacher.

Using the overhead transparency and the teacher lesson plan page, follow the instructional steps below to introduce each day's word or words.

1. **Pronounce** the word and point out the part of speech. Then have students say the word with you several times. If the word is long, pronounce it again by syllables, having students repeat after you.

2. **Read the definition** of the word; paraphrase using simpler or different language if necessary.

3. **Read the example sentence** and then have students read it with you. Discuss how the word is used in the sentence and ask questions to confirm understanding. For example: *We are waiting for a **definite** answer from Aunt Caitlin about when she is coming for a visit.* Ask: *What kind of answer would be a **definite** answer? What kind of answer would <u>not</u> be a **definite** answer?* Provide additional example sentences as necessary.

4. **Elaborate** on the meaning of the word using the suggestions on the teacher lesson plan page. These suggestions draw on common life experiences to illustrate the word meaning and give students opportunities to generate their own examples of use.

Teacher Resources

Transparency

part of speech and definition

example sentence

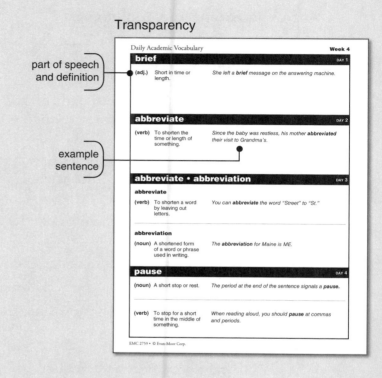

Teacher Lesson Plan

part of speech, definition, and example sentence as on transparency

teaching suggestions

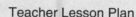
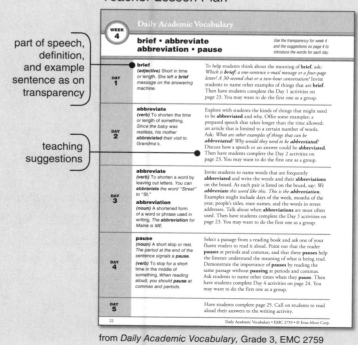

from *Daily Academic Vocabulary*, Grade 3, EMC 2759

Student Reproducibles

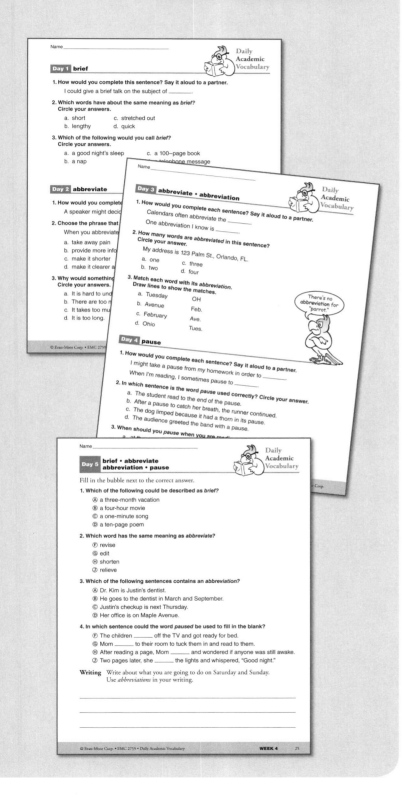

5. **Assess** students' understanding of the word(s) with the reproducible activities for Days 1 through 4.

   The first item is always an oral activity that is designed to be open-ended and answerable based on personal experience. You may wish to model a response before asking students to complete the item. Make sure that all students respond orally. Then call on a number of students to share their responses or those of a partner.

   Until students become familiar with the variety of formats used in the daily practice, you may wish to do the activities together as a class. This will provide support for English language learners and struggling readers.

6. **Review and assess** mastery of all the words from the week on Day 5. The review contains four multiple-choice items and a writing activity requiring students to use one or more of the week's words.

The instructional steps above were modeled after those presented by Kevin Feldman, Ed.D. and Kate Kinsella, Ed.D. in "Narrowing the Language Gap: The Case for Explicit Vocabulary Instruction," Scholastic Inc., 2004.

Review Week Walk-Through

Weeks 9, 18, 27, and 36 are review weeks. Each review covers all the words from the previous eight weeks.

Days 1–4

On Day 1 through Day 4 of the review weeks, students determine which academic vocabulary words complete a cloze paragraph.

Day 5

Day 5 of the review weeks alternates between a crossword puzzle and a crack-the-code puzzle.

Teacher Page

alphabetical list of the words to be reviewed

suggestions for ways to conduct review lessons

Extension ideas suggest ways to tie the words into subject area content.

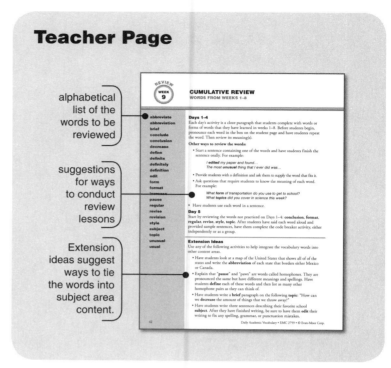

Student Reproducibles

Days 1–4

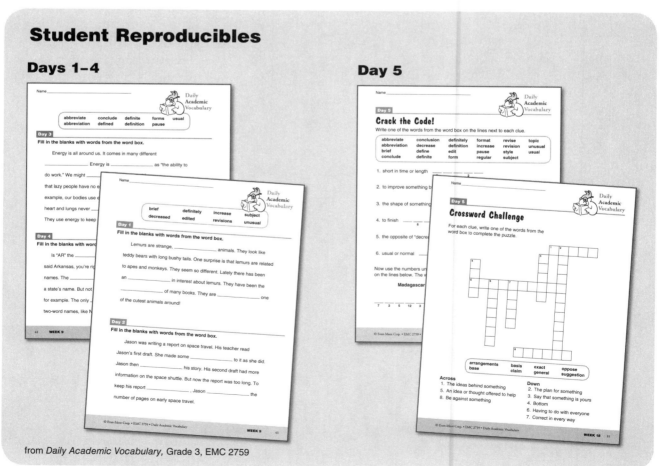

from *Daily Academic Vocabulary*, Grade 3, EMC 2759

Day 5

Meeting the Needs of English Language Learners

In addition to the direct, scaffolded instruction presented in *Daily Academic Vocabulary*, you may want to use some of the following sheltering strategies to assist English language learners in accessing the vocabulary.

Use Graphics
Draw a picture, a symbol, or other graphics such as word or idea maps to represent the word. Keep it simple. Then ask students to draw their own pictures. For example:

categorize   **similar**

Use Cognates with Spanish-Speaking Students
Cognates—words that are similar in meaning, spelling, and pronunciation—can make English more accessible for Spanish speakers. There are thousands of English words that have a related Spanish word. For example:

typical	típico
variety	variedad
combination	combinación

Model Correct Syntax and Usage in Oral Discussions
Model correct pronunciation. Use echoing strategies to teach correct usage and syntax. Teach the varied forms of words together, *agree* and *agreement* for example, to help students understand correct usage.

Provide Sentence Frames
For written activities, such as the final activity on all Day 5 pages, provide sentence starters or sentence frames that students can complete. For example:

*We knew that our study method was **effective** because…*

Teach Communication Strategies
Engaging in academic discussions requires a more formal language. Teach a variety of ways to begin responses when reporting or asking questions in class. For example:

Change this	To this
My partner said…	My partner shared/pointed out/indicated that…
That's not right!	I don't agree with you because…
I don't get it.	Will you explain that to me again?

subject • topic

Use the transparency for week 1 and the suggestions on page 6 to introduce the words for each day.

DAY 1

subject
(noun) An area of study, such as science. *Math is Greta's best **subject** in school.*

Have students name the different things they study in school—math, science, social studies, reading, language arts, health, music, art. Say: *Each of these things is a **subject** you study in school.* Invite students to talk about which school **subjects** they like best. After responses, ask: *Why do you like that **subject** the best?* Then have students complete the Day 1 activities on page 11. You may want to do the first one as a group.

DAY 2

subject
(noun) Someone or something that is thought about, written about, or talked about. *Our school picnic was the **subject** of a newspaper article.*

Display informational books that are familiar to students. Select books whose **subject** is suggested by the title—for example, Exploring the Night Sky or How a House Is Built. As you show each book, ask: *What is the **subject** of this book? What is it about?* Help them conclude that what a book is about is the **subject** of the book. Then have students complete the Day 2 activities on page 11. You may want to do the first one as a group.

DAY 3

topic
(noun) The subject of discussion or conversation. *Abigail always has a lot to say on the **topic** of dog care.*

Explain that **topic** and "subject" have very similar meanings and are sometimes used interchangeably. Say: *Something or someone can be the **topic** of discussion or the subject of discussion.* Ask: *What is our **topic** of discussion right now?* Read the sample sentence and ask: *Would the sentence have the same meaning if you replaced **topic** with the word "subject"?* Then have students complete the Day 3 activities on page 12. You may want to do the first one as a group.

DAY 4

topic
(noun) The subject of a book or other written work. *He has read many books on the **topic** of space travel.*

Say: *Both **topic** and "subject" are used to describe what a book or another piece of writing is about, as well as a discussion or conversation.* Ask a student to make up a sentence using the word **topic**. Then ask another student to repeat the sentence, substituting the word "subject" for **topic**. Ask: *Are the meanings of the two sentences the same?* Then have students complete the Day 4 activities on page 12. You may want to do the first one as a group.

DAY 5

Have students complete page 13. Call on students to read aloud their answers to the writing activity.

Day 1 subject

1. How would you complete this sentence? Say it aloud to a partner.

My idea of a hard subject is _____.

2. Which of these is <u>not</u> a *subject* you study in school? Circle your answer.

    a. math   c. bike riding

    b. spelling   d. science

3. In what *subject* would you study each of these things? Draw lines to match.

    a. the solar system   math

    b. subtraction   science

    c. our country's history   writing

    d. nouns and verbs   social studies

Day 2 subject

1. How would you complete this sentence? Say it aloud to a partner.

My favorite books are on the subject of _____.

2. The title of a book is <u>What's Out There: A Book About Space</u>. What is the *subject* of this book? Circle your answer.

    a. backyards   c. outer space

    b. empty rooms   d. woods and meadows

3. List three *subjects* that interest you.

    a. _____

    b. _____

    c. _____

One **subject** that interests me is ME!

Daily Academic Vocabulary

Day 3 | topic

1. How would you complete this sentence? Say it aloud to a partner.

I could say a lot about the topic of _____.

2. Which of these *topics* would you talk about in science class? Circle your answers.

    a. how magnets work   c. how plants grow
    b. a favorite TV show   d. nouns and verbs

3. Which sentence correctly uses the word *topic*? Circle your answer.

    a. They hiked to the topic of the mountain.
    b. They talked about a different topic every night.
    c. I like to topic about my favorite book.
    d. She took a topic to avoid getting the flu.

Day 4 | topic

1. How would you complete this sentence? Say it aloud to a partner.

I would be interested in an article on the topic of _____.

2. Which of these would make a good *topic* for a science report? Circle your answer.

    a. how I spent my summer vacation   c. how the president is elected
    b. how a caterpillar becomes a butterfly   d. how to make a turkey sandwich

3. Pretend that you are going to write a report. First, write the *topic* of your report. Then, write three things you would say about the *topic*.

Topic: My Dog   **Topic:** _____

    a. He likes to chase balls.   a. _____
    b. He has a big wet tongue.
    c. He sleeps on my bed.   b. _____

                                     c. _____

Name_____

Daily Academic Vocabulary

Day 5 **subject • topic**

Fill in the bubble next to the correct answer.

1. Which sentence could you complete with the word *subject*?

Ⓐ We have a different textbook for every _____.

Ⓑ Grandma's barn was the _____ for Barney's doghouse.

Ⓒ The librarian is a good _____ to help you find a book.

Ⓓ The dinosaur was _____ in the museum.

2. The *subject* of a book is _____.

Ⓕ a list of the chapters

Ⓖ a list of the topics covered in the book

Ⓗ what the book is about

Ⓙ the person who wrote the book

3. In which sentence could you replace the underlined word with the word *topic*?

Ⓐ A birthday is a good reason for celebration.

Ⓑ For some players, winning is the object of the game.

Ⓒ The dinner table is the perfect place for conversation.

Ⓓ Movies are Emma's favorite subject for discussion.

4. What is the *topic* of a news article entitled "California Feels the Heat"?

Ⓕ unusually cold weather in California

Ⓖ wood-burning stoves

Ⓗ hot weather in California

Ⓙ hot weather in Mexico

Writing Tell about the *subject* of a book you have read lately. Be sure to use the word *subject* in your writing.

edit • revise • revision

Use the transparency for week 2 and the suggestions on page 6 to introduce the words for each day.

DAY 1

edit
(verb) To check and correct errors in writing. *Before he handed it in, Rosemary edited Andrew's story.*

Write this sentence on the board, including errors: "The students is writing reports above kangeroos." Then say: *I need to edit what I just wrote.* Demonstrate the meaning of **edit** by correcting the errors in the sentence. Have students give the corrections. (Change "is" to "are"; change "above" to "about"; correct the spelling of "kangaroos.") Say: *We just edited this sentence.* Ask: *Why is it important to edit what you write?* Then have students complete the Day 1 activities on page 15. You may want to do the first one as a group.

DAY 2

revise
(verb) To make a piece of writing better by making it clearer or more correct. *The reporter will revise the newspaper article to include the new information.*

Write this sentence on the board: "I like fruit." Ask: *If we were going to revise this sentence to make it clearer and more correct, what kinds of changes might we make? How could we make it better?* Invite students to suggest ways to **revise** the sentence. (e.g., change "fruit" to "bananas"; insert "because they taste good and are a healthy snack") Then have students complete the Day 2 activities on page 15. You may want to do the first one as a group.

DAY 3

revision
(noun) A change that makes something better. *The revisions in word choice improved my sentences.*

Explain that **revision** is related to "revise." Write this sentence on the board: "Lions and tigers are cats." Using colored chalk or marker, insert the word "big" between the words "are" and "cats." Then say: *I made a revision to this sentence. The revision makes the sentence clearer and more correct. I made the revision with colored chalk (or marker).* Then have students complete the Day 3 activities on page 16. You may want to do the first one as a group.

DAY 4

revise
(verb) To change or make different. *He revised his plans when he saw the rain.*

Say: *Revise is also used when you make changes in things that are not written. For example, pretend that we had plans to go on a field trip to an art museum. However, something happened and the museum was closed that day. How could we revise our plans for the field trip?* Then have students complete the Day 4 activities on page 16. You may want to do the first one as a group.

DAY 5

Have students complete page 17. Call on students to read aloud their answers to the writing activity.

Daily Academic Vocabulary

Day 1 edit

1. How would you complete this sentence? Say it aloud to a partner.

It's important to edit your work to _____.

2. Which of the following things would you *edit*? Circle your answers.

a. a book report you wrote

b. a picture you painted

c. a model you built

d. a story you wrote

3. Which things might you do when you *edit*? Circle your answers.

a. write the first sentence

b. add a comma

c. correct a misspelled word

d. tape a torn page

Day 2 revise

1. How would you complete this sentence? Say it aloud to a partner.

When you revise a story that you wrote, you _____.

2. Why would you *revise* a book report? Circle your answers.

a. You are bored.

b. You forgot an important part.

c. You wrote the wrong title.

d. You want to type it on the computer.

3. Which sentence correctly uses the word *revise*? Circle your answer.

a. We will revise the computer.

b. We will revise the old house with paint.

c. We will revise the book to include new information.

d. We will revise what we learned to get ready for the test.

very
I am ᴧsmart.

Day 3 revision

1. How would you complete this sentence? Say it aloud to a partner.

I might make a revision to _____ because _____.

2. Which of the following is <u>not</u> an example of a *revision?* Circle your answer.

   a. adding new information

   b. adding a new sentence

   c. learning a poem by heart

   d. changing the order of words in a sentence

3. Which word has the same meaning as *revision?* Circle your answer.

   a. review   c. memory

   b. change   d. copy

Day 4 revise

1. How would you complete this sentence? Say it aloud to a partner.

Once my family had to revise our plans to _____.

2. In which sentence does someone *revise* something? Circle your answers.

   a. Sari would not listen to her friend.

   b. John changed his mind when he heard Jason's side of the story.

   c. Maria studied for her test.

   d. Angel wrote a story to read to the class.

3. Which phrase best completes this sentence? Circle your answer.

I revised my idea when _____.

   a. I kept it the same   c. I thought of something better

   b. I fell asleep   d. I read about it

Daily Academic Vocabulary

Day 5 **edit • revise • revision**

Fill in the bubble next to the correct answer.

1. Which sentence uses the word *edit* correctly?

    Ⓐ Always edit your pencil.

    Ⓑ Please edit your report before handing it in.

    Ⓒ Jeremy will edit the map to find out where we are.

    Ⓓ I will edit the paragraph by writing it neatly.

2. When you *revise* something, you _____ .

    Ⓕ make it clearer or more correct

    Ⓖ show your work

    Ⓗ copy it exactly as it was written

    Ⓙ read it out loud

3. In which sentence could *revision* be used to fill in the blank?

    Ⓐ She will _____ her last paragraph.

    Ⓑ This picture is a _____ of a famous painting.

    Ⓒ The new book is a _____ of a book written ten years ago.

    Ⓓ Always _____ your stories.

4. In which sentence could the underlined word <u>not</u> be replaced by *revise*?

    Ⓕ We need to <u>update</u> our thinking.

    Ⓖ You could <u>rethink</u> your views on the story.

    Ⓗ The plan is perfect, and we don't need to <u>change</u> it.

    Ⓙ Parents sometimes <u>preview</u> the movies their children want to see.

Writing Think about something you wrote for class recently. What is one thing you did to *revise* it? Be sure to use the word *revise* in your writing.

_____

_____

_____

usual • unusual • regular

Use the transparency for week 3 and the suggestions on page 6 to introduce the words for each day.

DAY 1

usual
(adj.) Normal, common, or expected. *We did the usual things that we do every day.*

Say: *Things or events that are **usual** are ones that we expect.* Ask: *What are some **usual** things you would see at school?* (e.g., students; pencils) *What are some **usual** activities that take place at school?* (e.g., students studying; eating lunch) Then have students complete the Day 1 activities on page 19. You may want to do the first one as a group.

DAY 2

unusual
(adj.) Not usual or ordinary. *It is very unusual for it to snow in Alabama.*

Say: *In the word **unusual**, the prefix "un-" was added to the word "usual." The prefix "un-" means "not," so **unusual** means "not usual."* Help students think about the meaning of **unusual** by naming a place (e.g., school; your backyard; a public park) and ask: *What would be **unusual** to see in this place? Why is it **unusual**?* Repeat with other places, helping students to name **unusual**, but not impossible, sightings. Then have students complete the Day 2 activities on page 19. You may want to do the first one as a group.

DAY 3

regular
(adj.) Usual or normal. *Vegetables should be a regular part of everyone's diet.*

Point out that **regular** and "usual" have nearly the same meanings. Say: *My usual lunch is a sandwich. My **regular** lunch is a sandwich. The meanings of the sentences are the same.* Ask a student to make a sentence using the word "usual." Have another student repeat the sentence, substituting **regular** for "usual." Ask: *Does changing the word change the meaning of the sentence? Why or why not?* Repeat this activity a few times. Then have students complete the Day 3 activities on page 20. You may want to do the first one as a group.

DAY 4

regular
(adj.) Always happening at the same time. *This bus makes regular trips to the library.*

Say: *Meals are **regular** if they are eaten at about the same time every day. Recess is a **regular** event because it happens at the same time every day. Tell me examples of things that are **regular**, that is, things that always happen at the same time.* After responses, ask: *What makes these things **regular**?* Then have students complete the Day 4 activities on page 20. You may want to do the first one as a group.

DAY 5

Have students complete page 21. Call on students to read aloud their answers to the writing activity.

Day 1 **usual**

1. How would you complete this sentence? Say it aloud to a partner.

The usual things I do after dinner are _____.

**2. Which of the following are *usual* activities at your school?
Circle your answers.**

   a. Teachers play on the swings.
   b. Students read books.
   c. The principal runs in the halls.
   d. Students draw pictures and do art projects.

**3. Which two words have about the same meaning
as *usual*? Circle your answers.**

   a. common   c. normal
   b. strange   d. helpful

A parrot is not your **usual** bird!

Day 2 **unusual**

1. How would you complete this sentence? Say it aloud to a partner.

It would be unusual to see _____ at school.

**2. Which of these animals would make an *unusual* pet?
Circle your answer.**

   a. cat   c. bear
   b. dog   d. hamster

**3. List three things that are usual things to see at a library
and three things that would be *unusual.***

Usual	Unusual
a. _____	a. _____
b. _____	b. _____
c. _____	c. _____

Day 3 regular

1. How would you complete this sentence? Say it aloud to a partner.

One of my regular chores is _____.

2. Which of these words means the opposite of *regular*? Circle your answer.

a. normal   c. usual

b. special   d. common

3. List three activities that are *regular* parts of your school day.

a. _____

b. _____

c. _____

Day 4 regular

1. How would you complete this sentence? Say it aloud to a partner.

We have regular _____ at school.

2. Which of the following things might be *regular*? Circle your answers.

a. visits to the library   c. trips to the supermarket

b. winning one million dollars   d. your ninth birthday

3. Which group of words best completes this sentence? Circle your answer.

Dentists want their patients to have regular _____.

a. sweets and desserts

b. afternoon naps

c. vacations at the beach

d. teeth cleanings

Name_____

Day 5 usual • unusual • regular

Fill in the bubble next to the correct answer.

1. In which sentence could *usual* take the place of the underlined word?

    Ⓐ Field Day was a <u>special</u> day for everyone.

    Ⓑ We did not follow our <u>everyday</u> activities.

    Ⓒ We learned lots of <u>new</u> games and fun activities.

    Ⓓ The day was very <u>different</u> and out of the ordinary.

2. Which word has the same meaning as *unusual*?

    Ⓕ normal

    Ⓖ unexpected

    Ⓗ common

    Ⓙ regular

3. In which sentence is the word *regular* <u>not</u> used correctly?

    Ⓐ Feeding the cat was one of her regular chores.

    Ⓑ The regular visitor had never been there before.

    Ⓒ The children got to stay up past their regular bedtime.

    Ⓓ Reading and writing are part of our regular classroom routine.

4. We have *regular* practice _____.

    Ⓕ on different days each week

    Ⓖ at different times each week

    Ⓗ at the same time each week

    Ⓙ whenever our coach thinks we need it

Writing Describe something *unusual* that happened to you.
Be sure to use the word *unusual* in your writing.

_____

_____

_____

Daily Academic Vocabulary

brief • abbreviate
abbreviation • pause

Use the transparency for week 4 and the suggestions on page 6 to introduce the words for each day.

DAY 1

brief
(adj.) Short in time or length. *She left a **brief** message on the answering machine.*

To help students think about the meaning of **brief**, ask: *Which is **brief**: a one-sentence e-mail message or a four-page letter? A 30-second chat or a two-hour conversation?* Invite students to name other examples of things that are **brief**. Then have students complete the Day 1 activities on page 23. You may want to do the first one as a group.

DAY 2

abbreviate
(verb) To shorten the time or length of something. *Because the baby was restless, his mother **abbreviated** their visit to Grandma's.*

Explore with students the kinds of things that might need to be **abbreviated** and why. Offer some examples: a prepared speech that takes longer than the time allowed; an article that is limited to a certain number of words. Ask: *What are other examples of things that can be **abbreviated**? Why would they need to be **abbreviated**?* Discuss how a speech or an answer could be **abbreviated**. Then have students complete the Day 2 activities on page 23. You may want to do the first one as a group.

DAY 3

abbreviate
(verb) To shorten a word by leaving out letters. *You can **abbreviate** the word "Street" to "St."*

abbreviation
(noun) A shortened form of a word or phrase used in writing. *The **abbreviation** for Maine is ME.*

Invite students to name words that are frequently **abbreviated** and write the words and their **abbreviations** on the board. As each pair is listed on the board, say: *We **abbreviate** this word like this. This is the **abbreviation**.* Examples might include days of the week, months of the year, people's titles, state names, and the words in street addresses. Talk about when **abbreviations** are most often used. Then have students complete the Day 3 activities on page 24. You may want to do the first one as a group.

DAY 4

pause
(noun) A short stop or rest. *The period at the end of the sentence signals a **pause**.*

(verb) To stop for a short time in the middle of something. *When reading aloud, you should **pause** at commas and periods.*

Select a passage from a reading book and ask one of your fluent readers to read it aloud. Point out that the reader **pauses** at periods and commas, and that these **pauses** help the listener understand the meaning of what is being read. Demonstrate the importance of **pauses** by reading the same passage without **pausing** at periods and commas. Ask students to name other times when they **pause**. Then have students complete Day 4 activities on page 24. You may want to do the first one as a group.

DAY 5

Have students complete page 25. Call on students to read aloud their answers to the writing activity.

 Daily Academic Vocabulary • EMC 2759 • © Evan-Moor Corp.

Name_____

Day 1 brief

1. How would you complete this sentence? Say it aloud to a partner.

I could give a brief talk on the subject of _____.

2. Which words have about the same meaning as *brief*? Circle your answers.

a. short   c. stretched out

b. lengthy   d. quick

3. Which of the following would you call *brief*? Circle your answers.

a. a good night's sleep   c. a 100-page book

b. a nap   d. a telephone message

Day 2 abbreviate

1. How would you complete this sentence? Say it aloud to a partner.

A speaker might decide to abbreviate her speech because _____.

2. Which phrase best completes this sentence? Circle your answer.

When you abbreviate something, you _____.

a. take away pain

b. provide more information

c. make it shorter

d. make it clearer and more complete

3. Why would something have to be *abbreviated*? Circle your answers.

a. It is hard to understand.

b. There are too many corrections.

c. It takes too much time.

d. It is too long.

Bye!

Day 3 abbreviate • abbreviation

1. How would you complete these sentences? Say them aloud to a partner.

Calendars often abbreviate the _____.

One abbreviation I know is _____.

2. How many words are *abbreviated* in this sentence? Circle your answer.

My address is 123 Palm St., Orlando, FL.

a. one   c. three

b. two   d. four

3. Match each word with its *abbreviation*.
Draw lines to show the matches.

a. Tuesday   OH

b. Avenue   Feb.

c. February   Ave.

d. Ohio   Tues.

There's no abbreviation for "parrot."

Day 4 pause

1. How would you complete these sentences? Say them aloud to a partner.

I might take a pause from my homework in order to _____.

When I'm reading, I sometimes pause to _____.

2. In which sentence is the word *pause* used correctly? Circle your answer.

a. The student read to the end of the pause.

b. After a pause to catch her breath, the runner continued.

c. The dog limped because it had a thorn in its pause.

d. The audience greeted the band with a pause.

3. When should you *pause* when you are reading aloud? Circle your answers.

a. at the end of a sentence   c. at the end of every line

b. after a long word   d. at a comma

Name _____

Daily
Academic
Vocabulary

Fill in the bubble next to the correct answer.

1. Which of the following could be described as *brief*?

   Ⓐ a three-month vacation

   Ⓑ a four-hour movie

   Ⓒ a one-minute song

   Ⓓ a ten-page poem

2. Which word has the same meaning as *abbreviate*?

   Ⓕ revise

   Ⓖ edit

   Ⓗ shorten

   Ⓙ relieve

3. Which of the following sentences contains an *abbreviation*?

   Ⓐ Dr. Kim is Justin's dentist.

   Ⓑ He goes to the dentist in March and September.

   Ⓒ Justin's checkup is next Thursday.

   Ⓓ Her office is on Maple Avenue.

4. In which sentence could the word *paused* be used to fill in the blank?

   Ⓕ The children _____ off the TV and got ready for bed.

   Ⓖ Mom _____ to their room to tuck them in and read to them.

   Ⓗ After reading a page, Mom _____ and wondered if anyone was still awake.

   Ⓙ Two pages later, she _____ the lights and whispered, "Good night."

Writing   Write about what you are going to do on Saturday and Sunday.
Use *abbreviations* in your writing.

_____

_____

_____

Daily Academic Vocabulary

WEEK 5

define • definition
definite • definitely

Use the transparency for week 5 and the suggestions on page 6 to introduce the words for each day.

DAY 1

define
(verb) To explain or tell the meaning of a word or phrase. *We **define** words when we tell what they mean.*

Write the word "agree" on the board. Have students read the word aloud. Then say: *I am going to **define** "agree." "Agree" means to think the same way.* Invite students to explain the meaning of "agree" in their own words. When students have suggested a meaning, say: *When you told me what the word "agree" means, you **defined** the word. What other words can you **define**?* Then have students complete the Day 1 activities on page 27. You may want to do the first one as a group.

DAY 2

definition
(noun) The meaning of a word or phrase. *The **definition** of "edit" is "to check for and correct errors in writing."*

Write the word "usual" on the board. Ask: *What does this word mean?* (normal; common) Work with students to come up with a **definition** of "usual" that the whole group agrees on. Write the **definition** on the board and read it aloud. Say: *We wrote a **definition** for "usual." Our **definition** tells what "usual" means.* Then have students complete the Day 2 activities on page 27. You may want to do the first one as a group.

DAY 3

definite
(adj.) Known for sure; certain. *We are waiting for a **definite** answer from Aunt Caitlin about when she is coming to visit.*

Write these two sentences on the board and read them aloud: *Annie said she will be here at 2 o'clock. Wendy said she could probably get here by 2:30.* Ask: *Which one of these sentences states something **definite**?* Have students suggest other sentences that state something **definite** and ones that do not state something **definite**. As each sentence is suggested, have the whole group decide if it makes a statement that is **definite** or not **definite**. Then have students complete the Day 3 activities on page 28. You may want to do the first one as a group.

DAY 4

definitely
(adv.) Without a doubt. *Jeremy will **definitely** finish his homework before bedtime.*

On the board, list a few things that have occurred so far in the school day. (e.g., bell; recess; lunch) Say: *These things have **definitely** happened.* Explore the meaning of **definitely** by having students tell things that will **definitely** happen. (e.g., leave school; go home; eat dinner) Then have students complete the Day 4 activities on page 28. You may want to do the first one as a group.

DAY 5

Have students complete page 29. Call on students to read aloud their answers to the writing activity.

---

26 — Daily Academic Vocabulary • EMC 2759 • © Evan-Moor Corp.

Name _____

Day 1 define

1. How would you complete this sentence? Say it aloud to a partner.

I would define the word "happy" as _____.

2. Which of these phrases *defines* the word "smooth"? Circle your answer.

    a. rocky point   c. rough or lumpy

    b. not rough   d. a calm sea

3. Which sentence correctly uses the word *define*? Circle your answer.

    a. Clare defined her garden with flowers and vegetables.

    b. Nina defined "brief" by saying it has the same meaning as "short."

    c. Elijah defined his cats Whiskers and Swishy Tail.

    d. Emil defined his invitation to the party.

Day 2 definition

1. How would you complete this sentence? Say it aloud to a partner.

Knowing the definitions for words is important when I read because _____.

2. Which of these words has about the same meaning as *definition*? Circle your answer.

    a. idea   c. meaning

    b. invention   d. feature

3. Match each of these words with its *definition*. Draw lines to show your answers.

    a. noticeable   the writer of a story, book, article, or play

    b. familiar   to have or own something

    c. author   able to be noticed or seen

    d. possess   well-known

Name_____

Daily Academic Vocabulary

Day 3 definite

1. How would you complete this sentence? Say it aloud to a partner.

My family has made definite plans to _____.

2. Which of the following things is most likely to be *definite*? Circle your answer.

    a. when you will be in school this week

    b. your vacation plans for the year 2030

    c. where you will go to college

    d. who will win a contest

3. In which sentence could the underlined word or words be replaced by the word *definite*? Circle your answer.

    a. It can be hard to <u>explain the meaning of</u> some words.

    b. Fred is <u>unsure</u> about his plans to go to the beach.

    c. The group came up with a <u>very original</u> answer to the problem.

    d. Amanda was not able to give a <u>certain</u> answer.

Day 4 definitely

1. How would you complete this sentence? Say it aloud to a partner.

Spinach pizza is definitely _____.

2. In which sentences is the word *definitely* used correctly? Circle your answers.

    a. Quentin was definitely about which books he liked.

    b. Ella could definitely use some help carrying the heavy box.

    c. Everyone decorated his or her mailbox definitely.

    d. He had studied hard and was definitely ready for the test.

3. Which two words have about the same meaning as *definitely*? Circle your answers.

    a. possibly   c. certainly

    b. believably   d. absolutely

I am **definitely** a funny parrot!

Name_____

Day 5 | **define • definition**
definite • definitely

Fill in the bubble next to the correct answer.

1. When you *define* a word, you _____.

    Ⓐ learn how to spell it

    Ⓑ write it neatly and carefully

    Ⓒ tell what it means

    Ⓓ say it without pausing

2. Which of these is a *definition* for "differently"?

    Ⓕ adjective

    Ⓖ four syllables

    Ⓗ noun

    Ⓙ in a way that is not the same

3. In which sentence could the word *definite* be used to fill in the blank?

    Ⓐ We have _____ plans to see a movie this weekend.

    Ⓑ The story was very dreamlike and _____.

    Ⓒ Because she was nervous, her voice sounded _____.

    Ⓓ She was not sure about her _____ answer.

4. The dog *definitely* needs a bath because _____.

    Ⓕ he hates getting wet

    Ⓖ he has long hair

    Ⓗ we bought some new dog shampoo

    Ⓙ he was rolling in the mud

Writing   Tell about something you will *definitely* do in the next week.
Be sure to use the word *definitely* in your writing.

_____

_____

_____

increase • decrease

Use the transparency for week 6 and the suggestions on page 6 to introduce the words for each day.

DAY 1

increase
(verb) To make greater or larger. *We will* **increase** *our classroom library by adding more books.*

Show students a stack of books. Then add more books to the stack. Say: *When I add more books to the stack, I* **increase** *the height of the stack, and I* **increase** *the number of books in the stack.* Invite students to suggest other things that can be **increased** in size or number and how that might be done. (e.g., trees; buildings; class) Then have students complete the Day 1 activities on page 31. You may want to do the first one as a group.

DAY 2

increase
(noun) A greater amount of something. *The movie theater announced an* **increase** *in the cost of a ticket.*

Tell students that **increase** can also be a thing or noun. Stack the books as you did for Day 1. Say: *When I add two more books to the stack, there is an* **increase** *of two books.* Ask students to name other things that might experience an **increase**. (e.g., number of students involved in sports; the number of students in a classroom; the number of cars in a parking lot) Then have students complete the Day 2 activities on page 31. You may want to do the first one as a group.

DAY 3

decrease
(verb) To make or become less. *Healthy habits can* **decrease** *the number of colds you get.*

Say: **Decrease** *is the opposite of "increase."* Show students the stack of books again. Say: *If I add more books, I increase the number of books in the stack.* Take away one book. Say: *If I remove one of the books, I* **decrease** *the number of books.* Ask students to suggest other things that could **decrease**. Then have students complete the Day 3 activities on page 32. You may want to do the first one as a group.

DAY 4

decrease
(noun) The amount by which something becomes less. *The flu caused a* **decrease** *in school attendance.*

Say: *As you now know, the words "increase" and* **decrease** *are opposites.* Show students the stack of books. Say: *There are books in this stack. If I added one book to the stack, would it be an increase or a* **decrease***?* Then ask: *If I took away one book, would that be an increase or a* **decrease***?* Then have students complete the Day 4 activities on page 32. You may want to do the first one as a group.

DAY 5

Have students complete page 33. Call on students to read aloud their answers to the writing activity.

Name _____

Day 1 increase

1. How would you complete this sentence? Say it aloud to a partner.

I want to increase my _____ collection.

2. Which phrase best completes this sentence? Circle your answer.

The school increased its size by _____.

a. painting it white   c. planting a garden

b. building more rooms   d. giving more homework

3. Which sentence correctly uses the word *increase*? Circle your answer.

a. Turning down the radio will increase the noise in your bedroom.

b. The air conditioner will increase the room.

c. Doing your math homework is likely to increase your score on the test.

d. Losing two players increased the size of our team.

Day 2 increase

1. How would you complete this sentence? Say it aloud to a partner.

I would like to ask for an increase in _____.

2. In which of the following would you like an *increase*? Circle your answers.

a. your allowance   c. bug bites

b. colds   d. your free time

3. Which amount shows an *increase* over the amount shown in the first glass? Circle the correct glass.

a.   b.   c.

Day 3 decrease

1. How would you complete this sentence? Say it aloud to a partner.

I want to decrease the _____.

2. Which word has about the same meaning as _decrease_? Circle your answer.

a. choose

c. increase

b. trick

d. reduce

3. Which sentence uses the word _decrease_ correctly? Circle your answer.

a. We can decrease the time we spend on this if we work faster.

b. Elliot tried to decrease us by not telling the truth.

c. When people move to our community, it decreases the population.

d. We add more water to the glass to decrease the amount.

Day 4 decrease

1. How would you complete this sentence? Say it aloud to a partner.

I would like to see a decrease in _____ because _____.

2. Which of these could cause a _decrease_ in your report card marks? Circle your answer.

a. studying

c. correct answers

b. neat writing

d. not doing your homework

3. In which of these things would a _decrease_ be a good thing? Circle your answers.

a. your allowance

b. littering

c. air pollution

d. the number of books you read

Say "NO" to a **decrease** in peanuts!

Name _____

Day 5 **increase • decrease**

Fill in the bubble next to the correct answer.

1. In which sentence is the word *increase* used correctly?

Ⓐ The cool breeze increased the heat.

Ⓑ A traffic jam increased the time it took to get to town.

Ⓒ Space travel increased the distance between the moon and Earth.

Ⓓ Studying increased his chances of failing the test.

2. An *increase* in the population means that _____.

Ⓕ there are more people

Ⓖ there are fewer people

Ⓗ people are taller

Ⓙ people live in many places

3. In which sentence could the word *decrease* be used to fill in the blank?

Ⓐ Reading teaches you new words and will _____ your vocabulary.

Ⓑ Exercise will _____ your level of fitness.

Ⓒ More children in school will _____ the need for teachers.

Ⓓ Since bats eat bugs, bats can _____ the insect population.

4. A *decrease* in rainfall could cause _____.

Ⓕ flooding

Ⓖ some plants to die

Ⓗ the rivers to rise

Ⓙ trees to grow faster

Writing Tell about something you would like to see *decreased*. Be sure to use the word *decrease* in your writing.

_____

_____

_____

form • format • style

Use the transparency for week 7 and the suggestions on page 6 to introduce the words for each day.

DAY 1

form
(noun) Type or kind. *Reading is Jared's favorite* **form** *of entertainment.*

Ask: *How can we get from one place to another?* (e.g., car; plane; train) Say: *Each of these is a* **form**, *or type, of transportation. Each is a different way to get from one place to another.* Invite students to name other **forms** of transportation. Then have students complete the Day 1 activities on page 35. You may want to do the first one as a group.

DAY 2

form
(verb) To make or create; give shape to. *How do we* **form** *a triangle?*

Say: *When I ask you to* **form** *your letters, I am asking you to make or create them.* Have several students come to the board. Ask each one to **form** a different letter. When each student finishes, ask the class: *What did (student's name)* **form**? Ask: *What else can we* **form** *with letters?* (e.g., words; sentences; stories) Then have students complete the Day 2 activities on page 35. You may want to do the first one as a group.

DAY 3

form
(verb) To make up or to organize. *Let's* **form** *a group to discuss this.*

Say: *The verb* **form** *also can be used to name actions where we organize in certain ways. We do this often in school. We might* **form** *small groups,* **form** *a line, or* **form** *two teams. What else might we* **form**? Then have students complete the Day 3 activities on page 36. You may want to do the first one as a group.

DAY 4

format
(noun) The way in which something is made up or organized. *The simple* **format** *of the game makes it easy to play.*

style
(noun) The way in which something is written, said, or done. *The writer's* **style** *is easy to understand.*

Show students two distinctly different books, such as one with pictures and captions, and one without any illustrations and of a different size. Ask: *What makes these two books different?* (e.g., one has pictures; one is true; one is larger) Say: *That is the* **format**. *The* **format** *of one book includes pictures; the other does not.* Then show students a silly storybook, such as one by Dr. Seuss. Say: *The* **style** *of something is the way in which something is written, such as funny or serious. What do you think the writing* **style** *of this book is?* (e.g., funny; silly) Encourage students to use the word **style** in their responses. Then have students complete the Day 4 activities on page 36. You may want to do the first one as a group.

DAY 5

Have students complete page 37. Call on students to read aloud their answers to the writing activity.

Day 1 form

1. How would you complete this sentence? Say it aloud to a partner.

My favorite form of fun is _____.

2. Which of the following are *forms* of exercise? Circle your answers.

a. playing soccer

b. riding the bus

c. riding a bicycle

d. watching a ballgame

3. Which word best completes this sentence? Circle your answer.

Fables are Navaeh's favorite form of _____.

a. flower   c. story

b. animal   d. music

Day 2 form

1. How would you complete this sentence? Say it aloud to a partner.

I can form clay into a _____.

**2. Which word or phrase best completes this sentence?
Circle your answer.**

Rain can form _____.

a. a sunny sky   c. mud puddles

b. trees   d. warm weather

**3. Which sentence correctly uses the word *form*?
Circle your answer.**

a. The bell forms loud and clear.

b. Marianne will form the cookie dough into heart shapes.

c. Flooding can be the form of too much rain.

d. King Kong forms the monster in our play.

I can **form** a nest out of wood.

Daily
Academic
Vocabulary

Day 3 form

1. How would you complete this sentence? Say it aloud to a partner.

I think it would be fun to form a _____ club.

2. What would people *form* to do each of these things?
Draw lines to show your answers.

a. to get on the bus   form a book club

b. to talk about books   form two teams

c. to play a basketball game   form a car pool

d. to take turns driving   form a line

3. Which sentence does <u>not</u> use the word *form* correctly? Circle your answer.

a. The students formed a circle for their reading group.
b. The gym teacher asked the students to form four teams.
c. Brad formed chocolate and milk to make chocolate milk.
d. Ramon formed a group to pick up the trash.

Day 4 format • style

1. How would you complete these sentences? Say them aloud to a partner.

The test format I like most is _____.

Our principal's speaking style is very _____.

2. Which of these things is part of newspaper's *format*? Circle your answers.

a. the size of the newspaper   c. how much the newspaper costs
b. who reads the newspaper   d. how much space is taken up with pictures

3. Which of these phrases describes an author's writing *style*?
Circle your answers.

a. uses white paper   c. drives an old car
b. makes you laugh out loud   d. uses long words

Daily
Academic
Vocabulary

Day 5 **form • format • style**

Fill in the bubble next to the correct answer.

1. Which of the following can be formed?

Ⓐ a poem

Ⓑ a ruler

Ⓒ a computer

Ⓓ a pencil

2. Which sentence does not use the word *form* correctly?

Ⓕ Jill formed jungle animals from clay.

Ⓖ The students formed a group to write a class newspaper.

Ⓗ The stones formed a bridge across the stream.

Ⓙ The book formed a story about an alligator.

3. Which of the following is not part of the *format* of a book?

Ⓐ the size of the pages

Ⓑ long sentences

Ⓒ the number of pictures

Ⓓ where the words appear on the page

4. Which of the following could have a funny *style*?

Ⓕ a desk

Ⓖ a story

Ⓗ a piece of paper

Ⓙ a potato chip

Writing   Describe your favorite *form* of after-school activity. Be sure to use the word *form* in your writing.

_____

_____

_____

conclude • conclusion

Use the transparency for week 8 and the suggestions on page 6 to introduce the words for each day.

DAY 1

conclude
(verb) To bring or come to an end. *The teacher **concluded** the lesson just as the recess bell rang.*

Say: *"To **conclude**" has the same meaning as "to end."* Write this sentence on the board and read it aloud: *The play will end with a dance number.* Erase "end" and write **conclude** in its place. Read the new sentence and ask: *Have I changed the meaning of this sentence by replacing "end" with **conclude**?* Then have students complete the Day 1 activities on page 39. You may want to do the first one as a group.

DAY 2

conclusion
(noun) The end or last part of something. *At the **conclusion** of the story, the lost dog found its way home.*

Choose a familiar story, such as a fairy tale. Show the book and say: *I am going to read you the **conclusion** of this story.* Read the last paragraph or two, and then say: *I read you the **conclusion** of the story.* Ask several students to tell the **conclusion** of a favorite story. Ask: *What other things have **conclusions**?* (e.g., movies; conversations) Then have students complete the Day 2 activities on page 39. You may want to do the first one as a group.

DAY 3

conclude
(verb) To decide based on the facts you have. *Henry looked at the paw print and **concluded** that it had been made by a cat.*

Say: ***Conclude** can also tell what you do when you make a decision after thinking about the facts or clues. If you walked into someone's home and saw a dog's leash and water bowl, what would you **conclude**?* After responses, say: *The leash and the water dish would help you **conclude** that the people who live there have a dog.* Give students other scenarios and ask what they would **conclude**. Then have students complete the Day 3 activities on page 40. You may want to do the first one as a group.

DAY 4

conclusion
(noun) A decision reached using the facts and clues you have. *We studied the clues and drew a **conclusion** about who had eaten the sandwich.*

Remind students of the scenario from Day 3. Say: *Seeing a dog's leash and water bowl helped you conclude that a dog lived in the house. You drew the **conclusion** that the people had a dog.* Say: *We often draw **conclusions** when we read by using facts from the story and things we already know to figure something out.* Ask: *Have you ever guessed the ending of a story before you read it all? In what book? You drew a **conclusion** based on what you had already read.* Then have students complete the Day 4 activities on page 40. You may want to do the first one as a group.

DAY 5

Have students complete page 41. Call on students to read aloud their answers to the writing activity.

Day 1 conclude

1. How would you complete this sentence? Say it aloud to a partner.

I like to conclude a friendly letter with _____.

2. In which sentence can the word *conclude* take the place of "end"?
Circle your answer.

    a. The coach will <u>end</u> his speech by saying, "Go team!"

    b. At the <u>end</u> of the game, we cheered our favorite team.

    c. Players and fans celebrated the <u>end</u> of a great season.

    d. In the <u>end</u>, having fun is more important than winning.

3. How might each of these things *conclude*? Draw lines to show your answers.

    a. a fairy tale   with the sun going down

    b. a tic-tac-toe game   with the audience clapping

    c. a concert   with one player getting three in a row

    d. a day   with "and they lived happily ever after"

Day 2 conclusion

1. How would you complete this sentence? Say it aloud to a partner.

I like story conclusions that are _____.

2. Which of these words means the opposite of *conclusion*? Circle your answer.

    a. end   c. beginning

    b. decision   d. partnership

3. In which sentence is the word *conclusion* <u>not</u> used correctly?
Circle your answer.

    a. In conclusion, I believe our school should recycle.

    b. At the conclusion of the recital, the dancers took a bow.

    c. At the conclusion of the school year, we celebrate with a party.

    d. At the conclusion of the school day, the bell rings to begin class.

Name _____

Day 3 conclude

1. How would you complete this sentence? Say it aloud to a partner.

Walking into my bedroom, someone could conclude that _____.

2. What might you *conclude* from each of the clues at the left?
Draw lines to show your answers.

a. cat hair on someone's clothes   It is raining outside.

b. people walking with open umbrellas   Someone is at the door.

c. someone yawns   The person has a cat.

d. the dog runs to the door and barks   The person needs a nap.

3. In which sentence could the underlined words be replaced by *conclude*?
Circle your answer.

a. Our national parks <u>take in</u> forests, mountains, and shorelines.
b. After listening to Tia, Ben had to <u>think</u> that she knew a lot about whales.
c. Hurrying caused Brianna to <u>leave out</u> a big part of the story.
d. Nicole and her sister never <u>agree</u> about anything.

Day 4 conclusion

1. How would you complete this sentence? Say it aloud to a partner.

When I smell food cooking at home, I come to the conclusion that _____.

2. Which phrase best completes this sentence? Circle your answer.

When I saw Ian carrying a stack of books, I drew the conclusion that _____.

a. he had lost his dog   c. the bookstore ran out of books
b. he had been to the library   d. he was trying to run faster

3. If you saw a bird with twigs in its beak, what *conclusion* might you draw?
Circle your answer.

a. Birds eat spiders.   c. It was summer.
b. There was a scarecrow nearby.   d. The bird was building a nest.

Daily Academic Vocabulary

Day 5 **conclude • conclusion**

Fill in the bubble next to the correct answer.

1. Which of these words does <u>not</u> have about the same meaning as *conclude*?

Ⓐ end

Ⓑ finish

Ⓒ complete

Ⓓ cover

2. Which of these things would most likely happen at the *conclusion* of a play?

Ⓕ The curtain would open.

Ⓖ The actors would bow.

Ⓗ The audience would take their seats.

Ⓙ The play would begin.

3. Which sentence does <u>not</u> use the word *conclude* correctly?

Ⓐ The school day will conclude at 3:00.

Ⓑ Let's conclude this book in our reading list.

Ⓒ The vet combed our dog's coat and concluded that he had fleas.

Ⓓ Looking at the puddles, Jake concluded that it had rained hard last night.

4. Which sentence best describes a *conclusion*?

Ⓕ A conclusion is a guess about what will happen next.

Ⓖ A conclusion is a creative idea about something you want to do.

Ⓗ A conclusion is an idea or decision based on what you know.

Ⓙ A conclusion is new idea that no one else has had.

Writing How would you like to *conclude* this school year? Be sure to use the word *conclude* in your writing.

_____

_____

_____

CUMULATIVE REVIEW
WORDS FROM WEEKS 1–8

abbreviate
abbreviation
brief
conclude
conclusion
decrease
define
definite
definitely
definition
edit
form
format
increase
pause
regular
revise
revision
style
subject
topic
unusual
usual

Days 1–4

Each day's activity is a cloze paragraph that students complete with words or forms of words that they have learned in weeks 1–8. Before students begin, pronounce each word in the box on the student page, have students repeat each word, and then review each word's meaning(s). **Other ways to review the words:**

- Start a sentence containing one of the words and have students finish the sentence orally. For example:

  I **edited** my paper and found…
  The most **unusual** thing that I ever did was…

- Provide students with a definition and ask them to supply the word that fits it.

- Ask questions that require students to know the meaning of each word. For example:

  What **form** of transportation do you use to get to school?
  What **topics** did you cover in science this week?

- Have students use each word in a sentence.

Day 5

Start by reviewing the six words not practiced on Days 1–4: **conclusion**, **format**, **regular**, **revise**, **style**, **topic**. Write the words on the board and have students repeat them after you. Provide a sentence for one of the words. Ask students to think of their own sentence and share it with a partner. Call on several students to share their sentences. Follow the same procedure for the remaining words. Then have students complete the code-breaker activity.

Extension Ideas

Use any of the following activities to help integrate the vocabulary words into other content areas:

- Have students look at a map of the United States that shows all the states and write the **abbreviation** of each state that borders either Mexico or Canada.

- Explain that "**pause**" and "paws" are words called homophones. They are pronounced the same but have different meanings and spellings. Have students **define** each of these words and then list as many other homophone pairs as they can think of.

- Have students write a **brief** paragraph on the following **topic**: "How can we **decrease** the amount of things that we throw away?"

- Have students write three sentences describing their favorite school **subject**. After they have finished writing, be sure to have them **edit** their writing to fix any spelling, grammar, or punctuation mistakes.

Daily Academic Vocabulary

brief	definitely	increase	subject
decreased	edited	revisions	unusual

Day 1

Fill in the blanks with words from the word box.

Lemurs are strange, _____ animals. They look like

teddy bears with long bushy tails. One surprise is that lemurs are related

to apes and monkeys. They seem so different. Lately there has been

an _____ in interest about lemurs. They have been the

_____ of many books. They are _____ one

of the cutest animals around!

Day 2

Fill in the blanks with words from the word box.

Jason was writing a report on space travel. His teacher read

Jason's first draft. She made some _____ to it as she did.

Jason then _____ his story. His second draft had more

information on the space shuttle. But now the report was too long. To

keep his report _____, Jason _____ the

number of pages on early space travel.

Daily Academic Vocabulary

abbreviate	conclude	definite	forms	usual
abbreviation	defined	definition	pause	

Day 3

Fill in the blanks with words from the word box.

Energy is all around us. It comes in many different _____.

Energy is _____ as "the ability to do work." We might

_____ from this _____ that lazy people have

no energy. But all living things use energy. For example, our bodies

use energy to keep us alive. Like machines, our heart and lungs never

_____, even when we are asleep. They use energy to keep

us running.

Day 4

Fill in the blanks with words from the word box.

Is "AR" the _____ for Arizona or Arkansas? If you

said Arkansas, you're right! It can be tricky to _____ state

names. The _____ pattern is to use the first two letters of

a state's name. But not all states follow this rule. Arizona is AZ,

for example. The only _____ rule is that for states with

two-word names, like New York, use the first letter of each word (NY).

Day 5

Crack the Code!

Write one of the words from the word box on the lines next to each clue.

abbreviate	conclusion	definitely	format	revise	topic
abbreviation	decrease	definition	increase	revision	unusual
brief	define	edit	pause	style	usual
conclude	definite	form	regular	subject	

1. short in time or length   __ __ __ __ __
   1 2

2. to improve something by making it clearer   __ __ __ __ __ __
   3

3. the shape of something   __ __ __ __
   4 5

4. to finish   __ __ __ __ __ __ __ __
   6 7 8

5. the opposite of "decrease"   __ __ __ __ __ __ __ __
   9 10 11

6. usual or normal   __ __ __ __ __ __ __
   12 13

Now use the numbers under the letters to crack the code. Write the letters on the lines below. The words will complete this sentence.

Madagascar is the only place in the world where _____.

__ __ __ __ __ __ __ __ __ __ __ __ __ __ __
7 2 5 12 3 11 10 13 9 1 2 4 6 12 9 8

arrange • arrangement arrangements

Use the transparency for week 10 and the suggestions on page 6 to introduce the words for each day.

DAY 1

arrange
(verb) To put into a specific order. *They will arrange the words in alphabetical order.*

Gather a number of books of different sizes and different types, both fiction and nonfiction. Say: *I can arrange these books in different ways. I can arrange them by size.* Demonstrate how that would be done. Then say: *I can arrange them into fiction and nonfiction.* Demonstrate that. Then ask: *Can you think of other ways to arrange these books?* (e.g., color; weight; alphabetical by title or author) Then have students complete the Day 1 activities on page 47. You may want to do the first one as a group.

DAY 2

arrangement
(noun) The way in which things are placed or grouped. *The arrangement of the desks made it easy to move around the room.*

Make an **arrangement** of items, such as blocks on a table or sticky notes on the board. Say: *I've made an arrangement of ___. Who would like to come up and make a different arrangement?* Invite a few students to change the **arrangement**. Each time, make a comment that includes the word **arrangement**, for example: *That's an interesting arrangement.* Then have students complete the Day 2 activities on page 47. You may want to do the first one as a group.

DAY 3

arrange
(verb) To make plans for or prepare. *Mr. Benson arranged for the class to visit the museum.*

To explore this meaning of **arrange**, say: *Imagine that we were going to arrange a trip to a zoo. What would we have to do to arrange a trip like that?* Have students suggest things that would be involved in **arranging** such a trip. As they suggest things, restate what is said using the word **arrange**. Then have students complete the Day 3 activities on page 48. You may want to do the first one as a group.

DAY 4

arrangements
(noun) The plans for something. *The librarian made the arrangements for a school book fair.*

Say: *The word arrangements has about the same meaning as "plans." You can make arrangements for a trip. You can make arrangements for a party.* Ask: *For what other things do you make arrangements?* Encourage students to use the word **arrangements** in their responses. Then have students complete the Day 4 activities on page 48. You may want to do the first one as a group.

DAY 5

Have students complete page 49. Call on students to read aloud their answers to the writing activity.

Day 1 arrange

1. How would you complete this sentence? Say it aloud to a partner.

I can arrange the clothes in my closet by _____.

2. Which sentences correctly use the word *arrange*? Circle your answers.

a. On the test, we had to arrange the words in alphabetical order.

b. Mieko will arrange the water in the pool.

c. Lionel carefully arranged the candles on the cake.

d. There was a huge arrange of food for the party.

3. Which words or phrases correctly complete this sentence? Circle your answers.

Books in the library are arranged by _____.

a. color   c. size

b. subject   d. author's last name

I arrange my bird seeds by size.

Day 2 arrangement

1. How would you complete this sentence? Say it aloud to a partner.

I could change the arrangement of my room by _____.

2. Which *arrangement* of shapes is the same as the first *arrangement*? Circle your answer.

       a.   b.   c.

3. Which sentence has the same words but in a different *arrangement*? Circle your answer.

Squirrels are there in the tree.

a. Is the squirrel in the tree?   c. The tree has squirrels in it.

b. Squirrels live in trees.   d. There are squirrels in the tree.

Day 3 arrange

1. How would you complete this sentence? Say it aloud to a partner.

I wish my teacher would arrange for _____.

2. In which sentence is *arranged* <u>not</u> used correctly? Circle your answer.

   a. Caitlin arranged to meet Nikia after school.

   b. Zoe's parents arranged for the baby sitter to come at 6:00.

   c. The children's ages arranged from 6 to 11.

   d. The Bartons arranged for someone to mow their lawn.

3. What might you *arrange* if you wanted to do each thing at the left? Draw lines to show your answers.

   a. celebrate someone's birthday   arrange a trip to the zoo

   b. see lions and tigers   arrange a trip to the vet

   c. have shorter hair   arrange a birthday party

   d. be sure your pet is healthy   arrange to get a haircut

Day 4 arrangements

1. How would you complete this sentence? Say it aloud to a partner.

I would like to make arrangements to _____ with my friends.

2. In which sentence can *arrangements* <u>not</u> replace the word "plans"? Circle your answer.

   a. Marianne's family <u>plans</u> to take a trip.

   b. All their travel <u>plans</u> are set.

   c. They made <u>plans</u> for a neighbor to feed the cat.

   d. They also made <u>plans</u> for the post office to hold their mail.

3. Which of these things require people to make *arrangements*? Circle your answers.

   a. carpooling   c. reading a book

   b. riding a bike   d. taking a trip on an airplane

Daily
Academic
Vocabulary

Day 5 **arrange • arrangement • arrangements**

Fill in the bubble next to the correct answer.

1. Which of these things could you *arrange*?

Ⓐ the wall of a building

Ⓑ the trees in a forest

Ⓒ the furniture in a room

Ⓓ the clouds in the sky

2. Which of these words has about the same meaning as *arrangement*?

Ⓕ pattern

Ⓖ reason

Ⓗ sound

Ⓙ apartment

3. Which of these sentences could you complete with the word *arrange*?

Ⓐ We will _____ the bus at the corner.

Ⓑ We will _____ for a bus to take us there.

Ⓒ We will _____ that the bus is here.

Ⓓ We will _____ by bus at 4:15.

4. In which sentence could the underlined word(s) be replaced by *arrangements*?

Ⓕ The school fair was the biggest <u>event</u> of the year.

Ⓖ The third grade was in charge of <u>making decorations</u> for the gym.

Ⓗ The fourth grade was in charge of the <u>entertainment</u>.

Ⓙ The parents' group made <u>plans</u> to have games and prizes.

Writing What would you like to *arrange* to do this weekend? Explain your ideas. Be sure to use the word *arrange* in your writing.

_____

_____

_____

Daily Academic Vocabulary

WEEK 11

base • basic
basics • basis

Use the transparency for week 11 and the suggestions on page 6 to introduce the words for each day.

DAY 1	**base** *(noun)* The lowest part of something or the part something stands on. *Moss grew at the **base** of the tree.*	Show students a lamp or some other object in the room that has a **base**. Point to the **base** and explain that **base** and "bottom" have almost the same meaning. Say: *A **base** is what a thing rests on or the part that something stands on.* Then draw a picture of a mountain on the board. Say: ***Base** can also mean the lowest part of something.* Ask: *Where is the **base** of this mountain?* Then have students complete the Day 1 activities on page 51. You may want to do the first one as a group.
DAY 2	**base** *(verb)* To use as a starting point for something else. *She will **base** her story on an actual event.*	Remind students of a nursery rhyme, such as "Mary Had a Little Lamb." Then ask: *If we **base** a story on this rhyme, what are some things that might happen in the story?* Say: *These events could be part of a story that is **based** on ("Mary Had a Little Lamb").* Ask: *Can you think of any movies that are **based** on a book?* Then have students complete the Day 2 activities on page 51. You may want to do the first one as a group.
DAY 3	**basic** *(adj.)* Forming the main part of something. *Jayden explained the **basic** idea of the game.* **basics** *(noun)* The most important skills or facts to know. *Ruby has mastered the **basics** of horseback riding.*	Choose a game that you know all your students play and understand. Ask: *What is the **basic** idea of the game? What is the point or object of the game?* Then ask: *What are the **basics** of the game? What are the most important things you need to know in order to play this game?* Have students explain the skills that are the **basics** of the game. Encourage students to use the words **basic** and **basics** in their responses. Then have students complete the Day 3 activities on page 52. You may want to do the first one as a group.
DAY 4	**basis** *(noun)* The reasons or ideas behind something. *Kelly's idea became the **basis** for the whole plan.*	Say: *The **basis** of something is what it is built on or what it develops from. The **basis** for friendships is often shared interests, or things you both like. Think about your friends.* Ask: *What do you think is the **basis** of your friendship with the person you consider your best friend?* Then have the students complete the Day 4 activities on page 52. You may want to do the first one as a group.
DAY 5		Have students complete page 53. Call on students to read aloud their answers to the writing activity.

50

Daily Academic Vocabulary • EMC 2759 • © Evan-Moor Corp.

Name_____

Day 1 base

1. How would you complete this sentence? Say it aloud to a partner.

Something in our classroom that has a base is _____.

2. Which one is the *base* of the statue? Circle the letter.

a.—————→

c.—————→

←——— b.

←——— d.

3. Which phrase best completes this sentence? Circle your answer.

The children _____ around the base of the tree.

a. looked up at the bird's nest

b. climbed on the branches

c. raked the fallen leaves

d. saw birds fly

Day 2 base

1. How would you complete this sentence? Say it aloud to a partner.

I have seen a movie that was based on a _____.

2. Match the book titles to what they are *based* on.
Draw lines to show your answers.

a. The Big Plant

b. Emily and the Enchanted Frog

c. When I Was Young in the Mountains

d. How Lion Became King of the Animals

"The Frog Prince"

the author's own life

an African folk tale

"Jack and the Beanstalk"

3. What would not happen in a movie *based* on real life? Circle your answers.

a. Bicycles would fly.

b. It would take place in Kansas.

c. It would be about the past.

d. A scarecrow would come to life.

Day 3 basic • basics

1. How would you complete these sentences? Say them aloud to a partner.

The basic ingredients of my favorite snack are _____.

The basics of riding a bicycle are _____.

2. Which of these is <u>not</u> a *basic* skill you learn in school? Circle your answer.

a. number facts   c. spelling words

b. letters and sounds   d. kite flying

3. Think of a game or sport you know. List the *basics* for playing it.

Topic: soccer   **Game or Sport:** _____

a. dribbling

b. passing   a. _____

c. receiving

     b. _____

     c. _____

Day 4 basis

1. How would you complete this sentence? Say it aloud to a partner.

The basis of the story I have written is _____.

2. Which of these words does <u>not</u> have about the same meaning as *basis*? Circle your answer.

a. starting point   c. basement

b. cause   d. reason

3. Which sentence could you complete with *basis*? Circle your answer.

a. We can store the wood in the _____.

b. Grandpa taught Xavier the _____ skills of fishing.

c. Amanda's suggestion was the _____ of our group's report.

d. Flowers were planted at the _____ of the flagpole.

Daily Academic Vocabulary

Day 5 **base • basic • basics • basis**

Fill in the bubble next to the correct answer.

1. Which phrase does <u>not</u> tell the meaning of *base*?

Ⓐ the lowest part

Ⓑ the bottom

Ⓒ what something stands on

Ⓓ under the ground

2. Which of the following would a writer be most likely to *base* a story on?

Ⓕ a math problem

Ⓖ a funny thing that happened

Ⓗ a writing desk

Ⓙ a piece of paper

3. Which of the following is <u>not</u> a *basic* skill needed to do crossword puzzles?

Ⓐ knowledge of words

Ⓑ knowledge of word meanings

Ⓒ ability to subtract

Ⓓ ability to spell words correctly

4. Which of the following would probably <u>not</u> be a *basis* for a school project?

Ⓕ wanting to learn about sharks

Ⓖ preparing for the field trip to a museum

Ⓗ talking on the phone

Ⓙ discovering a fossil

Writing Tell about something you would like to *base* a story on. Be sure to use the word *base* in your writing.

_____

_____

_____

oppose • opposite

Use the transparency for week 12 and the suggestions on page 6 to introduce the words for each day.

DAY 1

oppose
(verb) To be against something. *I'm sure the principal will oppose our idea to have a longer recess.*

Say: *If you are against something, you oppose it.* Ask: *What is something that you are opposed to?* (e.g., cruelty to animals; too much homework; tests) *Why do you oppose it? What can you do to show that you oppose it?* Then have students complete the Day 1 activities on page 55. You may want to do the first one as a group.

DAY 2

opposite
(noun) Something or someone that is completely different from another. *Hot is the opposite of cold.*

(adj.) As different as possible. *They had opposite opinions of the book.*

Draw a large square and a small square on the board. Say: *This square is large. This square is small. "Large" is the opposite of "small"; the squares are opposites. What is the opposite of "front"?* (back) Say: *Yes, "front" and "back" have opposite meanings.* Repeat with other simple **opposites**. (top–bottom; in–out) Each time say: *Yes, ___ and ___ have opposite meanings.* Then have students complete the Day 2 activities on page 55. You may want to do the first one as a group.

DAY 3

opposite
(adj.) Facing away or moving the other way. *The library and the office are in opposite directions from our room.*

Ask two students to stand back-to-back in front of the class. Have them both walk forward, away from each other. Say: *(Student 1) and (Student 2) are walking in opposite directions.* Then ask the students to turn around and walk back toward where they started. Say: *Now each person is going the opposite way.* Have two other students do the same thing. Ask the class: *How would you describe the direction in which these students are walking?* (**opposite**) Then have students complete the Day 3 activities on page 56. You may want to do the first one as a group.

DAY 4

opposite
(adj.) Located directly across; on the other end or side. *We sat on opposite ends of the park bench.*

Choose two students who are sitting in **opposite** positions in the room. (front–back; **opposite** sides) Say: *___ and ___ are sitting on opposite ends/sides of the room.* Repeat the activity with several pairs of students. Then guide students in making statements about other things in the school or room that are **opposite** each other. Have students complete the Day 4 activities on page 56. You may want to do the first one as a group.

DAY 5

Have students complete page 57. Call on students to read aloud their answers to the writing activity.

Name_____

Day 1 oppose

1. How would you complete this sentence? Say it aloud to a partner.

My parents are opposed to me _____.

2. Think about the people listed at the left. What would each group *oppose*? Draw lines to show your answers.

a. animal lovers   cutting down forests

b. people who love trees   litter

c. people who clean up parks and beaches   the library closing

d. people who love to read   being mean to animals

3. Which of these things are you *opposed* to? Circle your answers.

a. longer school days   c. extra homework

b. no summer vacation   d. staying up past your bedtime

Day 2 opposite

1. How would you complete these sentences? Say them aloud to a partner.

_____ and _____ are opposites.

My friend and I have opposite opinions about _____.

2. For each word, write a word that means the *opposite*.

a. happy   _____

b. remember   _____

c. easy   _____

d. multiply   _____

What is the **opposite** of "quiet"?

3. Which two objects have *opposite* purposes? Circle your answer.

a. a cup and a glass   c. a pencil and an eraser

b. a radio and a CD player   d. a coat and a jacket

Day 3 opposite

1. How would you complete this sentence? Say it aloud to a partner.

From our classroom, _____ and _____ are in opposite directions.

2. Which arrows are pointing in *opposite* directions? Circle your answers.

    a.   b.   c.   d.

3. Which sentence describes people who are going in *opposite* directions? Circle your answer.

    a. Amelia and Tara jogged side by side.

    b. Brandon's little brother tagged along behind him.

    c. Eliot turned right at the corner, and Colin went left.

    d. Ellen walked so fast that Henry had a hard time keeping up.

Day 4 opposite

1. How would you complete this sentence? Say it aloud to a partner.

My home is on the opposite side of the street from _____.

2. Complete each sentence with the phrase that makes sense. Draw lines to show your answers.

    a. Anna and Tad walked on opposite   City Hall.

    b. The library is on the opposite corner from   side of the room.

    c. Tia waved to Gus from the opposite   ends of the table.

    d. The king and queen sat at opposite   sides of the street.

3. Which sentence correctly uses the word *opposite*? Circle your answer.

    a. The riverbank runs opposite to the river.

    b. The two hotels are on opposite ends of the park.

    c. The people are opposite to higher gas prices.

    d. Gigi's parents opposite her from seeing scary movies.

Daily Academic Vocabulary

Day 5 **oppose • opposite**

Fill in the bubble next to the correct answer.

1. Which sentence uses the word *oppose* correctly?

Ⓐ Peter sat at the table opposed to door.

Ⓑ The word "private" is opposed to "public."

Ⓒ People are opposed to tearing down the old hotel.

Ⓓ The lion statues are on opposed sides of the door.

2. Which word is the *opposite* of "shout"?

Ⓕ yell

Ⓖ whisper

Ⓗ scream

Ⓘ shouted

3. If two people walk in *opposite* directions, _____.

Ⓐ one walks fast and the other walks slow

Ⓑ one follows the other

Ⓒ one walks forward and the other walks behind

Ⓓ one goes left and the other goes right

4. If Jaime and Xander live in *opposite* parts of town, which sentence might be true?

Ⓕ Jaime and Xander both live close to the school.

Ⓖ Jaime lives north of town, and Xander lives east of town.

Ⓗ Jaime and Xander ride the bus to school.

Ⓘ Jaime lives in the north of town, and Xander lives in the south of town.

Writing   What is something you are *opposed* to? Explain why you *oppose* it. Be sure to use the word *oppose* in your writing.

_____

_____

_____

sum • total
summary • summarize

Use the transparency for week 13 and the suggestions on page 6 to introduce the words for each day.

DAY 1	**sum** *(noun)* A number that you get by adding two or more numbers. *The **sum** of 5 and 8 is 13.*	Write this addition problem on the board: 3 + 4 = 7. Say: *When you add 3 and 4, you get 7. 7 is the **sum** of 3 and 4.* Write other addition problems on the board. Each time, have students identify the **sum**. Then have students complete the Day 1 activities on page 59. You may want to do the first one as a group.
DAY 2	**total** *(noun)* The whole amount. *A **total** of 50 states are in the United States.* *(adj.)* Making up the whole amount. *The **total** population of the world is 6.5 billion.*	Point out that **total** means about the same thing as "sum." Say: *You add numbers together to find the sum. You also add things together to find the **total**.* Ask: *What is the **total** number of students in this room?* Explain that "sum" is usually used only to refer to the answer in an addition problem, but **total** is used more generally. (e.g., the **total** population or the **total** cost of something) Ask: *What is the **total** number of desks (or tables) in this room?* Then have students complete the Day 2 activities on page 59. You may want to do the first one as a group.
DAY 3	**total** *(verb)* To find the sum of numbers. ***Total** the number correct before turning in your quiz.*	Write these numbers in a column on the board: 2, 3, 4, 5. Ask: *If I asked you to **total** these numbers, what would you do?* Point out that as a verb, **total** has the same meaning as "add." Then have students complete the Day 3 activities on page 60. You may want to do the first one as a group.
DAY 4	**summary** *(noun)* A short statement giving the main points of something that has been written or spoken. *Leah gave a **summary** of what the principal said in her speech.* **summarize** *(verb)* To give the main points of something that has been written or spoken. *All students **summarized** their book reports for the class.*	Mention a story or fairy tale that you know is familiar to all the students and give a short account of the story. Then say: *I just **summarized** (story title). I gave you a **summary** of the story.* Ask a student to **summarize** a story with which you know he or she is familiar. Then ask: *When else would things be **summarized**?* Help the students think of times they might **summarize** something. (e.g., telling a story; talking about a vacation; describing a movie or book) Ask: *Why would you need to **summarize** it? Why would having a **summary** of something be useful?* Encourage students to use the words **summary** and **summarize** in their responses. Then have students complete the Day 4 activities on page 60. You may want to do the first one as a group.
DAY 5		Have students complete page 61. Call on students to read aloud their answers to the writing activity.

Name_____

Daily Academic Vocabulary

Day 1 sum

1. How would you complete this sentence? Say it aloud to a partner.

The sum of _____ and _____ is _____.

2. Which number in this number sentence is the *sum*? Circle your answer.

12 + 31 + 17 = 60

a. 17   c. 12
b. 60   d. 31

3. In which sentence could you use *sum* to fill in the blank? Circle your answer.

a. Gabriela divided 24 by 8 to get the _____ of 3.
b. Justin subtracted 57 from 83 to get the _____ of 26.
c. Chloe multiplied 7 by 9 to get the _____ of 63.
d. Rashid added 10, 81, and 37 to get the _____ of 128.

Day 2 total

1. How would you complete these sentences? Say them aloud to a partner.

So far this week, I have read a total of _____.

I would like to know the total number of people who _____.

2. Which number is the *total* of these shapes? Circle your answer.

a. 4   c. 2
b. 3   d. 1

3. The *total population* of the class is 17 students. Which phrase has about the same meaning as the underlined words? Circle your answer.

a. the sum of all the girls in the class
b. the number of students in the school
c. the sum of all the students in the class
d. the number of students living on Earth

Daily Academic Vocabulary

Day 3 total

1. How would you complete this sentence? Say it aloud to a partner.

I can total the number of _____ in my classroom.

2. Which problem requires that you *total*? Circle your answer.

a. $8 - 3$ c. $7 - 4$

b. 2×5 d. $3 + 5$

3. In which sentence can *total* replace the word "add"? Circle your answer.

a. Ben wanted to <u>add</u> toppings to the pizza.

b. Mom reminded him it would <u>add</u> to the cost.

c. The waiter will <u>add</u> all the charges.

d. Mom will <u>add</u> a tip to the final bill.

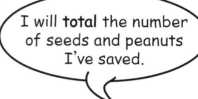

I will **total** the number of seeds and peanuts I've saved.

Day 4 summary • summarize

1. How would you complete these sentences? Say them aloud to a partner.

I could give a summary of _____.

I can summarize my weekend by _____.

2. Which phrase best completes this sentence? Circle your answer.

Mateo will summarize the book _____.

a. before reading it   c. before checking it out of the library

b. in his book report   d. by reading it on vacation

3. Which of the following things is <u>not</u> true about a *summary*? Circle your answer.

a. It is short.   c. It tells every detail.

b. It tells the main ideas.   d. It includes only what is important.

Daily Academic Vocabulary

Day 5 sum • total • summary • summarize

Fill in the bubble next to the correct answer.

1. Which problem has an answer that is a *sum*?

Ⓐ 12 − 7 = _____

Ⓑ 3 × 4 = _____

Ⓒ 8 + 10 = _____

Ⓓ 15 − 2 = _____

2. In which sentence could *sum* take the place of *total*?

Ⓕ Karin wanted to know the total number of pets in her class.

Ⓖ She found out the total dog population.

Ⓗ She would total that with the number of cats, fish, and gerbils.

Ⓙ The total would be all her classmates' pets.

3. When you *total* a set of something you _____.

Ⓐ order them from least to greatest

Ⓑ add them all together

Ⓒ find the average

Ⓓ group the odd and even numbers

4. Which of these things would you probably <u>not</u> *summarize*?

Ⓕ a book

Ⓖ pictures

Ⓗ a speech

Ⓙ a story

Writing *Summarize* your favorite memory. Describe what happened. Be sure to use the word *summary* or *summarize* in your writing.

_____

_____

_____

model • copy

Use the transparency for week 14 and the suggestions on page 6 to introduce the words for each day.

DAY 1

model

(noun) A small version of something. *We built a model of a volcano in science class.*

(verb) To use something as the plan or idea for something else. *Lucy modeled her cat painting after her pet Fluffy.*

Show students a toy airplane or car, a stuffed animal, and a baby doll. Say: *All of these objects are models. They were modeled after larger things. They are like the bigger versions, but they are not exactly the same.* Invite students to find other things in the classroom that are **modeled** after something. (e.g., a globe; a diorama) Then have students complete the Day 1 activities on page 63. You may want to do the first one as a group.

DAY 2

model

(adj.) Ideal or perfect. *Tomás is a model citizen because he is nice to people, helps out in the community, and obeys the law.*

Help students think about what makes something or someone a **model**, or ideal, example. Start a discussion by asking questions such as: *What words would describe a model student?* (e.g., studies hard) *A model athlete?* (e.g., strong; fast) *Who would you model yourself after?* Then have students complete the Day 2 activities on page 63. You may want to do the first one as a group.

DAY 3

copy

(noun) Something that looks or sounds exactly like another thing. *The museum built the dinosaur using copies of the original bones.*

(noun) One of a number of things that were printed at the same time. *Angel brought a copy of his favorite book to class.*

Point out that a **copy** is different from a model. A model is made to represent, or look like, something else, but a **copy** is meant to look exactly like the original thing. Show students a photocopy of a worksheet. Ask: *Is this paper a model or a copy?* Next, have students show you a specific textbook. Say: *Each of you has a copy of this book. They are all the same. They were printed at the same time. What other things do you have a copy of?* Then have students complete the Day 3 activities on page 64. You may want to do the first one as a group.

DAY 4

copy

(verb) To write down the same way. *After the teacher writes the question on the board, we copy it onto our papers.*

(verb) To do the same as somebody or something else. *The monkeys in the zoo copied my funny faces.*

Write a short sentence on the board and then ask students to write it down on a piece of paper. Say: *You have just copied a sentence. The sentence you wrote is the same as the sentence on the board.* Point out that actions can also be **copied**, or imitated. Parrots, for example, **copy** the words that they hear spoken by people. Then have students complete the Day 4 activities on page 64. You may want to do the first one as a group.

DAY 5

Have students complete page 65. Call on students to read aloud their answers to the writing activity.

Daily Academic Vocabulary

Day 1 model

1. How would you complete these sentences? Say them aloud to a partner.

I would like to make a model of a _____.

I could model a sand castle after _____.

2. Which of the following are *models* of something larger?
Circle your answers.

a. a baby doll

c. a garbage truck

b. a toy railroad set

d. a library

3. Which sentence correctly uses the word *model*? Circle your answer.

a. They modeled the tree after a seed.

b. Some people model their cars after the color red.

c. Trinity modeled her painting after one she had seen in a book.

d. Alyssa modeled her hair after curls.

Day 2 model

1. How would you complete this sentence? Say it aloud to a partner.

I think a _____ is a model pet because _____.

2. Which word or words might describe a *model* teacher? Circle your answers.

a. fair

c. forgetful

b. forgiving

d. hard to understand

3. Think of a *model* person and list three words that describe him or her.

Person: nurse

a. calm

b. friendly

c. caring

Person: _____

a. _____

b. _____

c. _____

Name_____

Day 3 copy

1. How would you complete these sentences? Say them aloud to a partner.

Once in the classroom, I made a copy of _____.

I can find a copy of the _____ in the library.

2. Which shape is a *copy* of the first shape? Circle your answer.

a.   b.   c.

3. Which phrase best completes this sentence? Circle your answer.

Isabella brought a copy of _____ to school.

a. her dog   c. the newspaper
b. the ball   d. her new hat

Day 4 copy

1. How would you complete these sentences? Say them aloud to a partner.

My teacher asked us to copy _____.

I think it's fun to copy the sounds made by a _____.

2. Which phrase best completes this sentence? Circle your answer.

I like to copy the _____.

a. tree growing in the yard   c. blue car driving on the road
b. tall building in the city   d. barking sounds made by the dog

3. Which of the following might you *copy* from the board onto a piece of paper? Circle your answers.

a. a sentence   c. a marker
b. a poem   d. an eraser

Daily
Academic
Vocabulary

Day 5 **model • copy**

Fill in the bubble next to the correct answer.

1. Which sentence uses the word *model* correctly?

Ⓐ I was asked to model the letter and send it to Aaron.

Ⓑ Joshua's pet cat Lucy is a model of a lion.

Ⓒ There was a model of the spaceship in the museum.

Ⓓ Each student had a model of the book.

2. An important quality of a *model* singer is _____.

Ⓕ being small

Ⓖ being able to sing in tune

Ⓗ having red hair

Ⓙ knowing other singers

3. In which sentence could the word *copy* be used to fill in the blank?

Ⓐ Every student received a _____ of the book.

Ⓑ The Ice King 2.0 is the latest _____ of refrigerator.

Ⓒ A globe is a _____ of the Earth.

Ⓓ A _____ student always turns in her homework.

4. In which sentence could the underlined words be replaced by the word *copy*?

Ⓕ The toy airplane was a <u>small version</u> of the big jet.

Ⓖ Amy was the <u>ideal</u> helper at home.

Ⓗ Emma used her dream as the <u>idea</u> for a new story.

Ⓙ We tried to <u>write down</u> the words exactly as they were printed.

Writing Describe something that you have *copied* or have seen a *copy* of. Be sure to use the word *copy* in your writing.

_____

_____

_____

suggest • suggestion • claim

Use the transparency for week 15 and the suggestions on page 6 to introduce the words for each day.

DAY 1

suggest
(verb) To offer something as an idea. *I suggest that we watch a movie.*

suggestion
(noun) An offered idea or thought. *It was Darin's suggestion to go hiking.*

Ask: *Imagine we could do anything we wanted this afternoon. What would you suggest we do? Tell me your suggestions.* Have students respond by saying, "I suggest we ___," or "My suggestion is ___." Then say: *I asked you to suggest what we could do this afternoon. Many of you made interesting suggestions.* Then have students complete the Day 1 activities on page 67. You may want to do the first one as a group.

DAY 2

suggest
(verb) To give a hint of something else or offer clues. *Dark clouds suggest that it might rain.*

Say: *Suggest means to give a clue. Things can suggest.* Ask: *If I came to school with a cast on my arm, what would that suggest to you? What would you think happened?* Have students share their ideas, using the phrase, "A cast suggests that ___." Then ask: *What would suggest that a plant needs water? What would suggest that no one is home at a house?* Encourage students to use the word suggest in their responses. Then have students complete the Day 2 activities on page 67. You may want to do the first one as a group.

DAY 3

claim
(verb) To say that something is true. *Amanda claims that her dog had eleven puppies.*

Say: *If I say you are the best group of kids in school, I claim you're the best. If I claim something, I say it is true.* Ask students to make statements they think are true. Have another student restate what a student says using the word claim. For example, a student might say, "I am a good speller." Another student would say: "(Student's name) claims he (or she) is a good speller." Then have students complete the Day 3 activities on page 68. You may want to do the first one as a group.

DAY 4

claim
(verb) To get something or to say that something is yours. *The best speller will claim first place at the spelling bee.*

Say: *You can claim that something is true. You can also claim that something is yours—that you own it or that you earned it.* Ask: *What kinds of things might you claim?* (e.g., praise or credit; a prize; a good seat on the bus) Have students respond by saying, "I can claim ___." Then have students complete the Day 4 activities on page 68. You may want to do the first one as a group.

DAY 5

Have students complete page 69. Call on students to read aloud their answers to the writing activity.

Day 1 **suggest • suggestion**

1. How would you complete these sentences? Say them aloud to a partner.

My parents will often suggest _____.

I try to follow my teacher's suggestion to _____.

2. Which phrase best completes this sentence? Circle your answer.

If you suggest hamburgers for dinner, you _____.

a. help make them   c. say you would like them

b. order them   d. eat two of them

3. Which of these statements is a *suggestion*? Circle your answer.

a. Come over here right now!   c. Will's mom took us to the video store.

b. Where are we going?   d. You should see The Wizard of Oz.

Day 2 **suggest**

1. How would you complete this sentence? Say it aloud to a partner.

My school desk suggests that I _____.

2. In which sentence could *suggest* take the place of the underlined words? Circle your answer.

a. Dishes in the sink <u>are a clue</u> that they need to be washed.

b. Clean hands and enough sleep <u>are ways to prevent</u> colds.

c. Apples and grapes <u>are examples of</u> healthy snacks.

d. Two Dr. Seuss books <u>are on my list of</u> books to read.

3. Each action on the left *suggests* a statement on the right. Draw lines to show the matches.

a. lots of scratching   The neighbors are going on a trip.

b. putting suitcases in the car   The woman has more than one cat.

c. buying a big bag of cat food   The person is in a hurry.

d. walking fast   The dog has fleas.

Daily Academic Vocabulary

Day 3 | claim

1. How would you complete this sentence? Say it aloud to a partner.

My friend claims that _____.

2. Which of the following would a scientist <u>not</u> *claim*? Circle your answers.

   a. Pollution is bad for the Earth.
   b. Sitting too close to the TV could hurt your eyes.
   c. Exercise is not good for you.
   d. Candy is a healthy food.

3. What might someone who loves math *claim*? Circle your answer.

   a. I hate math.
   b. I'm a good math student.

   c. Math is boring.
   d. I'd rather do anything than study math.

Day 4 | claim

1. How would you complete this sentence? Say it aloud to a partner.

One thing I claim credit for at home is _____.

2. Which of the following would someone <u>not</u> want to *claim*?
Circle your answer.

   a. blame for doing something bad
   b. credit for doing something good
   c. first prize in a contest
   d. a reward for finding a lost pet

3. Which phrase best completes this sentence?
Circle your answer.

Because no one claimed the coat, _____.

   a. it was black
   b. it fell on the floor
   c. it went in the lost and found box
   d. it was everyone's favorite

I'll **claim** the coat if no one else wants it!

Day 5 suggest • suggestion • claim

Fill in the bubble next to the correct answer.

1. Which sentence could you complete with the word *suggest*?

Ⓐ Our teacher expects us to _____ our homework.

Ⓑ Our teacher asked us to _____ new books to read.

Ⓒ Our teacher asked us to _____ our parents' permission.

Ⓓ Our teacher reminded us to _____ our names on our work.

2. Which sentence uses the word *suggestion* correctly?

Ⓕ Marcus drew a suggestion of the stars.

Ⓖ Bibi didn't keep her suggestion to help.

Ⓗ It was Sam's suggestion to do the project on stars.

Ⓙ A scary story might suggestion a small child.

3. Gray skies and people carrying umbrellas *suggest* that it is _____.

Ⓐ time to play outside

Ⓑ time go sledding

Ⓒ hot and sunny

Ⓓ raining

4. In which sentence is the word *claim* <u>not</u> used correctly?

Ⓕ Melissa claims she is an excellent skater.

Ⓖ Lionel claimed credit for winning the game.

Ⓗ Josh claimed to the teacher yesterday.

Ⓙ Avery claimed the idea was his.

Writing Where would you like to go for your next class field trip? Tell where you would like to go and why. Use the word *suggest* or *suggestion* in your writing.

_____

_____

_____

Daily Academic Vocabulary

WEEK 16

event • occur • occurrence

Use the transparency for week 16 and the suggestions on page 6 to introduce the words for each day.

DAY 1

event
(noun) Something that happens, especially something interesting or important. *Field Day is a big event at our school.*

List on the board **events** at your school or in your community that are important and familiar to students. Say: *These are events that take place in our community.* Then ask: *Why do we call these events? What makes them so special or important?* Then have students complete the Day 1 activities on page 71. You may want to do the first one as a group.

DAY 2

occur
(verb) To take place or happen. *Thunderstorms often occur during the summer.*

Point out that **occur** has the same meaning as "happen." Write this sentence on the board: "Your birthday happens every year." Have students read it aloud. Then replace "happens" with **occurs**. Ask: *Have I changed the meaning of the sentence? Does it still make the same statement? What are other events that often occur?* Then have students complete the Day 2 activities on page 71. You may want to do the first one as a group.

DAY 3

occur
(verb) To come to mind. *Ideas often occur to me while I'm reading.*

Say: ***Occur** can also describe when things come to mind, or that you thought of them. Sometimes things **occur** to you because of something you see. Look around the room. What **occurs** to you when you look at something?* Model this for the students. (e.g., *When I see the papers on my desk, it **occurs** to me that I need to grade them.*) Encourage students to use the word **occur** in their responses. Then have students complete the Day 3 activities on page 72. You may want to do the first one as a group.

DAY 4

occurrence
(noun) Something that takes place. *Snow is a common winter occurrence in Switzerland.*

Point out that **occurrence** and "event" both mean something that happens. Often they can be used interchangeably, but not always. An "event" is usually something special or important. An **occurrence** is often something ordinary that happens regularly. Then ask: *Would you call the arrival of the school bus an event or an **occurrence**? Would you call a school picnic an event or an **occurrence**? What is a regular **occurrence** at school?* (e.g., reading; working; lunch) Then have students complete the Day 4 activities on page 72. You may want to do the first one as a group.

DAY 5

Have students complete page 73. Call on students to read aloud their answers to the writing activity.

Daily Academic Vocabulary • EMC 2759 • © Evan-Moor Corp.

Daily Academic Vocabulary

Day 1 | event

1. How would you complete this sentence? Say it aloud to a partner.

So far, the biggest event for me this year was _____.

2. Which of these things would you consider an *event?* Circle your answers.

   a. a parade   c. a band concert

   b. a discussion in class   d. playing tag on the playground

3. List three *events* that happen in your community.

   a. _____

   b. _____

   c. _____

Day 2 | occur

1. How would you complete this sentence? Say it aloud to a partner.

_____ occurs every week.

2. In which sentence can *occur* <u>not</u> take the place of the underlined word or words? Circle your answer.

   a. The meeting will <u>take place</u> at 4:00 p.m.

   b. Recess breaks <u>happen</u> at the same time every day.

   c. The clerk asked everyone to <u>take a place</u> in line.

   d. How did these mistakes <u>come about</u>?

3. List three things that you know will *occur* in the next two days.

   a. _____

   b. _____

   c. _____

Daily Academic Vocabulary

Day 3 occur

1. **How would you complete this sentence? Say it aloud to a partner.**

    When I woke up today, it occurred to me that _____.

2. **Which sentence can you complete with the word *occur*? Circle your answer.**

    a. Frieda _____ an idea for a project.

    b. Ideas often _____ to her on a walk.

    c. On the walk home, she _____ an idea.

    d. Now she must _____ it to her teammates.

3. **Which of these things might suddenly *occur* to you? Circle your answers.**

    a. a book report

    b. the idea for a story

    c. a map of the world

    d. what something reminds you of

Day 4 occurrence

1. **How would you complete this sentence? Say it aloud to a partner.**

    _____ is a common occurrence in my home.

2. **Which phrase best completes this sentence? Circle your answer.**

    Celebrations are a regular occurrence _____.

    a. on Mondays

    b. for one person

    c. on holidays

    d. for people who hate noise

3. **Which word means about the same thing as *occurrence*? Circle your answer.**

    a. exit

    b. disagreement

    c. event

    d. memory

Flying is a regular **occurrence** for me!

Day 5 event • occur • occurrence

Fill in the bubble next to the correct answer.

1. Which sentence could you <u>not</u> complete with the word *event*?

Ⓐ The school play is a big _____ in the school year.

Ⓑ A birthday party is a special _____.

Ⓒ At the end of the game, the scores were _____.

Ⓓ The county fair was the biggest _____ of the summer.

2. The longest day of the year always *occurs* _____.

Ⓕ in winter

Ⓖ in summer

Ⓗ when it's night

Ⓙ on Saturday

3. Which sentence could you complete with the word *occurred*?

Ⓐ The idea _____ to her to start a club.

Ⓑ Liang _____ playing soccer every day.

Ⓒ Brianna _____ her idea with the rest of the class.

Ⓓ The thought of swimming in the river _____ him.

4. In which sentence could the word *event* be replaced by *occurrence*?

Ⓕ The parade is a major <u>event</u> in our town.

Ⓖ They are planning a special <u>event</u> to celebrate the day.

Ⓗ A full moon is a regular <u>event</u>.

Ⓙ A visit from Grandma was a big <u>event</u> at Hoon's house.

Writing Tell about an *event* that you are looking forward to. Be sure to use
the word *event* in your writing.

_____

_____

_____

general • generalize
generalization • exact • exactly

Use the transparency for week 17 and the suggestions on page 6 to introduce the words for each day.

DAY 1

general
(adj.) Having to do with everybody or everything. *There was **general** interest in going to the water park.*

Say: *Imagine that we were trying to decide on a class project. If everyone wanted to do the same thing, there would be **general** agreement. If everyone wanted to do something different, there would be **general** disagreement.* Explore some class issues on which there is **general** agreement or disagreement. Then have students complete the Day 1 activities on page 75. You may want to do the first one as a group.

DAY 2

general
(adj.) Having to do with only the main parts or ideas. *Wendy gave us a **general** idea of what we had to do for the party.*

generalize
(verb) To form a rule from a small number of specific examples. *The teacher can **generalize** that her students know addition from their high test scores.*

Say: *I am going to be very busy working around the house this weekend. That gave you a **general** idea of my plans for the weekend. Notice that I didn't tell you specific things I would be doing.* Ask: *Can you give me a **general** idea of your plans for the weekend?* (e.g., relax; travel; play) Then say: *When we **generalize**, we make a broad statement about something using facts. We can **generalize** that our school is very ___.* (e.g., friendly; clean) *This does not mean that everything is that way, but we can show that many things are.* Ask: *What can we **generalize** about our class?* Then have students complete the Day 2 activities on page 75. You may want to do the first one as a group.

DAY 3

generalization
(noun) A statement or idea that is general, or not specific. *Saying that dogs like riding in cars is a **generalization**.*

Write this sentence on the board: "Students like books about kids their own age." Read the sentence aloud and say: *This sentence is a **generalization**. It tells something that might be generally true but may not be true about every student in the world. What other **generalizations** do adults make about kids?* Then have students complete the Day 3 activities on page 76. You may want to do the first one as a group.

DAY 4

exact
(adj.) Correct and right in every way. *We know the **exact** number of people in the play.*

exactly
(adv.) In the correct or right way. *Franco's answer was **exactly** right.*

Explain that **exact** is in some ways the opposite of "general." Say: *Use **exact** and **exactly** when there can be no other answer. For example, the **exact** number of students in our class is ___. There are **exactly** ___ students in our class.* Then ask: *How is knowing **exactly** what is expected of you different from having a general idea about what you're going to do? Which would you rather have for a school project, an **exact** idea or a general idea?* Then have them complete the Day 4 activities on page 76. You may want to do the first one as a group.

DAY 5

Have students complete page 77. Call on students to read aloud their answers to the writing activity.

Name _____

Day 1 general

1. How would you complete this sentence? Say it aloud to a partner.

Our class showed general agreement about _____.

2. Which of the following would show *general* surprise?
Circle your answer.

    a. Someone fainted.

    b. Everyone's mouths dropped open.

    c. A few people clapped their hands.

    d. Several people laughed.

3. In which sentence is the word *general* <u>not</u> used correctly?
Circle your answer.

    a. One student's grade proves general improvement for the whole class.

    b. Class art supplies are for general use.

    c. There was general support for planting more trees.

    d. The new cafeteria menu was met with general approval.

Day 2 general • generalize

1. How would you complete these sentences? Say them aloud to a partner.

I have only a general idea about _____.

From my homework scores, I can generalize that _____.

2. Which of these parts of a book can give you a *general* idea of what a book is about? Circle your answers.

    a. title of the book   c. the author's name

    b. cover of the book   d. color of the cover

3. What can you *generalize* about schools? Circle your answer.

    a. Yours is the best.   c. Some have art programs.

    b. They help you learn.   d. You have to go to school.

Day 3 generalization

1. How would you complete this sentence? Say it aloud to a partner.

It is a generalization to say that all dogs _____.

2. Which of these sentences is a *generalization?* Circle your answer.

   a. Jason read a book about lizards.
   b. A gecko is a kind of lizard.
   c. All lizards eat insects.
   d. Akiko has a pet lizard.

3. Which of these statements is true about a *generalization?* Circle your answers.

   a. It makes a general statement.
   b. It talks about just one person or thing.
   c. It tells all the facts.
   d. It may not be true for everyone or everything.

Day 4 exact • exactly

1. How would you complete these sentences? Say them aloud to a partner.

My exact address is _____.

I was exactly right when I _____.

2. Which pattern is an *exact* copy of the pattern in the box? Circle your answer.

□ ○ △ □   □ ○ □ △   □ ○ ▽ □   □ ○ △ □
                a.   b.   c.

3. Which sentence correctly uses the word *exactly?* Circle your answer.

   a. Vito guessed that path was exactly 7 miles long.
   b. Maura knew that she had exactly $2.73 in her pocket.
   c. Bianca gave us a general idea of exactly what she wanted.
   d. Because the sun was high in the sky, Tim figured it was exactly noon.

Name_____

Day 5 | general • generalize • generalization
exact • exactly

Fill in the bubble next to the correct answer.

1. When there is a *general* understanding, _____.

   Ⓐ most people think the same thing

   Ⓑ some people tell others how they feel

   Ⓒ a few people might have the same opinion

   Ⓓ no one knows very much

2. If someone gets the *general* idea, she _____.

   Ⓕ understands all the facts completely

   Ⓖ finds out what everyone else knows

   Ⓗ gets the basic idea

   Ⓙ agrees with everybody else

The **exact** number of feathers I have is 4,726!

3. Which sentence is a *generalization*?

   Ⓐ Some teachers are nice.

   Ⓑ My teacher is funny.

   Ⓒ All teachers are strict.

   Ⓓ Many teachers like to travel.

4. In which sentence could the word *exactly* be used to fill in the blank?

   Ⓕ The plane arrived at _____ 8:24 p.m.

   Ⓖ When fully grown, he thinks this puppy will weigh _____ 60 pounds.

   Ⓗ He couldn't see the clock, but he thought it was _____ 3 o'clock.

   Ⓙ He guessed that the drive would take _____ half an hour.

Writing What is something that people *generalize* about kids that you think is wrong? Why do you think it is wrong? Be sure to use the word *generalize* in your writing.

_____

_____

_____

CUMULATIVE REVIEW
WORDS FROM WEEKS 10–17

arrange
arrangement
arrangements
base
basic
basics
basis
claim
copy
event
exact
exactly
general
generalization
generalize
model
occur
occurrence
oppose
opposite
suggest
suggestion
sum
summarize
summary
total

Days 1–4

Each day's activity is a cloze paragraph that students complete with words or forms of words that they have learned in weeks 10–17. Before students begin, pronounce each word in the box on the student page, have students repeat each word, and then review each word's meaning(s). **Other ways to review the words:**

- Start a sentence containing one of the words and have students finish the sentence orally. For example:

    *We made **arrangements** to…*
    *It is not a good idea to **copy**…*

- Provide students with a definition and ask them to supply the word that fits it.

- Ask questions that require students to know the meaning of each word. For example:

    *How would you **summarize** what we did yesterday?*
    *How can you prove that something is **exactly** two inches long?*
    *Name some **events** that happen in our community.*

- Have students use each word in a sentence.

Day 5

Start by reviewing the words in the crossword activity for Day 5. Write the words on the board and have students repeat them after you. Provide a sentence for one of the words. Ask students to think of their own sentence and share it with a partner. Call on several students to share their sentences. Follow the same procedure for the remaining words. Then have students complete the crossword activity.

Extension Ideas

Use any of the following activities to help integrate the vocabulary words into other content areas:

- Have students write a **summary** to **suggest** a school **event** sponsored by your class. What are the **basics** of the **event**? What **arrangements** would have to be made? Choose one **event** and make it happen!

- To check for comprehension, ask students to **summarize** what they learned at the end of a social studies or science lesson.

- Have students **suggest** ways to make a **model** of your country. Then have them create the **models**.

- Have students use measuring tools to find the **exact** measurements of various classroom objects. Have them write a **summary** of their findings.

**Daily
Academic
Vocabulary**

arrangement	basics	occur	sum
basic	exactly	suggest	total

Day 1

Fill in the blanks with words from the word box.

You can use clouds to do _____ weather forecasting.

The shape and _____, or grouping, of clouds can

help you predict what the weather will be. Clouds that look like rows of

fuzzy bubbles _____ that cold weather is coming. If it is

warm and humid, big clouds with flat tops tell you that a thunderstorm

may _____.

Day 2

Fill in the blanks with words from the word box.

Adding is one of the _____ of math. When you add,

you _____ numbers to find the _____.

When you add, you should always check your answer to be sure it

is _____ right. You can use a calculator to check your

answers. Answers can't be "almost right" when you add.

Name_____

| arrange | generalization | occurrence | summarize | copies |
| modeled | opposite | summary | events | |

Day 3

Fill in the blanks with words from the word box.

When you _____ a story, you tell the main ideas of

the story. You tell who the characters are. You tell what the problem is.

Then you retell the important _____. You should describe

each _____ in the order in which it happened. Your

_____ should give someone who hasn't read the story

a good idea of what happens and why.

Day 4

Fill in the blanks with words from the word box.

Ms. Pearson's class decided to _____ the furniture

to make a Reading Corner. They _____ the space after

a corner in the public library. They stocked the bookshelves with their

favorite books and _____ of children's magazines. They

placed three beanbag chairs _____ the bookshelves.

We can make a _____ that everyone loves the

Reading Corner!

Day 5

Crossword Challenge

For each clue, write one of the words from the word box to complete the puzzle.

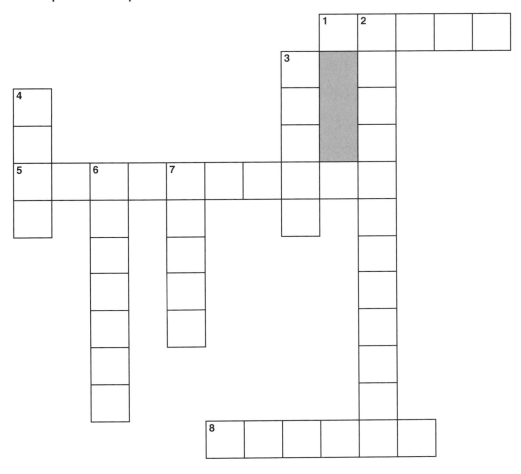

arrangements	basis	exact	oppose
base	claim	general	suggestion

Across

1. the ideas behind something
5. an idea or thought offered to help
8. to be against something

Down

2. the plan for something
3. to say that something is yours
4. bottom
6. having to do with everyone
7. correct in every way

consider • decide • decision

Use the transparency for week 19 and the suggestions on page 6 to introduce the words for each day.

DAY 1

consider
(verb) To think about something carefully. *The class will consider many topics before choosing one to write on.*

Ask one student this question: *What is your favorite book? Please think carefully and consider your answer before telling me.* As the student prepares to respond, make the comment that the student is **considering** what he or she is going to say. Ask other students different questions, each time telling them to "carefully **consider**" their answers. Then ask: *When would it be important to consider something before you do or say it?* Then have students complete the Day 1 activities on page 83. You may want to do the first one as a group.

DAY 2

consider
(verb) To believe to be true. *Many people consider our school to be the best in the city.*

Ask: *What do you consider to be the best thing about this year?* Have students respond with, "I **consider** ___." Then ask: *What do you consider to be the best movie?* Again, encourage students to use the word **consider** in their responses. Then have students complete the Day 2 activities on page 83. You may want to do the first one as a group.

DAY 3

decide
(verb) To make up your mind about something. *Our teacher decides which books we will read for book reports.*

Show students three books. Say: *If I ask you to choose one of these books to read, I am asking you to decide which book you would like to read. Which would you decide to read? Why did you decide on that book?* Ask: *What are things you decide each day?* (e.g., what to wear; what to eat for lunch; what to do during recess) Then have students complete the Day 3 activities on page 84. You may want to do the first one as a group.

DAY 4

decision
(noun) A final choice or judgment. *Our group discussed the choices before making a decision.*

Say: *When you decide something, you make a decision.* Ask several students: *What is a decision you have recently made? What helped you make your decision? Was it hard to make a decision? Why?* Reinforce the term each time by encouraging students to use the word **decision** in their answers. Then have students complete the Day 4 activities on page 84. You may want to do the first one as a group.

DAY 5

Have students complete page 85. Call on students to read aloud their answers to the writing activity.

Day 1 consider

1. How would you complete this sentence? Say it aloud to a partner.

When I choose a book to read, I consider _____.

2. Which of these things must you *consider* when you do a word problem in math? Circle your answers.

    a. what you need to find out

    b. if all the words are spelled right

    c. how many words are in the problem

    d. if you need to add, subtract, multiply, or divide

3. Which phrase best completes this sentence? Circle your answer.

When you consider your choices, you _____.

    a. can't decide what to do   c. do the first thing that comes to mind

    b. think hard before deciding   d. decide not to do anything

Day 2 consider

1. How would you complete this sentence? Say it aloud to a partner.

I consider math to be _____.

2. Which sentence can you complete with *consider?* Circle your answer.

    a. Audra and Kim _____ math more than science.

    b. Dipak would _____ read than do anything else.

    c. Teachers always _____ Husna to write more.

    d. What do you _____ to be your best subject in school?

3. Tell what you *consider* to be each of the following. Write your answers on the lines.

    a. the best book _____

    b. the best movie _____

    c. the best sport _____

Daily Academic Vocabulary

Day 3 | decide

1. How would you complete this sentence? Say it aloud to a partner.

To decide what to do after school, I will _____.

2. Which of these things can you *decide* for yourself? Circle your answers.

 a. what you will be taught today

 b. whether you will have homework

 c. what ice-cream flavor is your favorite

 d. what is in your book report

3. Which sentence does <u>not</u> use the word *decide* correctly? Circle your answer.

 a. The book group will decide which book to read next.

 b. The judges will decide who the winner is.

 c. They flipped a coin to decide which movie to see.

 d. Teachers decide students to make an effort.

Day 4 | decision

1. How would you complete this sentence? Say it aloud to a partner.

When I have to make a decision, I _____.

2. Which of the following are ways to make a *decision*? Circle your answers.

 a. voting   c. choosing

 b. arguing   d. not thinking about it

3. Which one does <u>not</u> require making *decisions*? Circle your answer.

 a. ordering a pizza   c. painting a picture

 b. following directions   d. getting dressed for school

Wearing this hat was a good **decision!**

Daily Academic Vocabulary

Day 5 **consider • decide • decision**

Fill in the bubble next to the correct answer.

1. If you *consider* a problem, it means that you _____.

Ⓐ think hard about it

Ⓑ try to avoid it

Ⓒ make things hard for others

Ⓓ use math to figure it out

2. If you *consider* something to be a problem, it means that you _____.

Ⓕ do it in math

Ⓖ make up your mind about it

Ⓗ think it's troublesome or hard

Ⓙ made it up yourself

3. Which sentence can you complete with the word *decide*?

Ⓐ Kirsten will _____ Soo Ha to be her partner.

Ⓑ They will _____ a social studies project.

Ⓒ First they need to _____ on a topic to study.

Ⓓ Then they will read to _____ about their topic.

4. Which of the following is a *decision* that you can make?

Ⓕ when the sun comes up

Ⓖ whether or not it rains

Ⓗ what you do in your free time

Ⓙ when school is over for the day

Writing   What is the hardest *decision* you have ever made? Be sure to use one of this week's words in your writing.

_____

_____

_____

attempt • fail • failure

Use the transparency for week 20 and the suggestions on page 6 to introduce the words for each day.

DAY 1

attempt
(verb) To try to do something. *Colin will* **attempt** *to stand on his head.*

Place a trash can about 15 feet from you. Show students three paper wads. Say: *I am going to* **attempt** *to throw these paper wads in the trash can.* Take your shots, but miss. Then say: *I* **attempted** *to make the baskets. How did I do?* Point out that **attempt** has about the same meaning as "try." Say: *When you* **attempt** *to do something, you try to do it. What is something you would like to* **attempt**? Then have students complete the Day 1 activities on page 87. You may want to do the first one as a group.

DAY 2

attempt
(noun) An effort to try to do something. *Anna's first* **attempt** *to hit the ball was a success!*

Bring out the paper wads and trash can again. Say: *Today I'm going to make another* **attempt** *to throw these into the can.* Take your shots, but miss again. Then ask: *Was that* **attempt** *successful or not?* Point out that just like the word "try," **attempt** can be a verb or a noun. Then have students complete the Day 2 activities on page 87. You may want to do the first one as a group.

DAY 3

fail
(verb) To try to do something and not be able to do it. *You may* **fail** *the first time, but don't give up.*

Bring out the paper wads and trash can again. Say: *Today I'm going to attempt the shots again. Will I succeed or* **fail**? Shoot and miss. Then ask: *Did I succeed, or did I* **fail**? Explain that when you **fail**, you are not able to do the thing you set out to do. Then ask: *What is something you* **failed** *at on your first attempt, but now do well?* Then have students complete the Day 3 activities on page 88. You may want to do the first one as a group.

DAY 4

failure
(noun) Someone or something that is not successful. *Monty's first attempt to fly a kite was a* **failure**.

Bring out the paper wads one more time. Place the trash can across the room. Say: *I'm going to attempt to throw these one more time.* Make another unsuccessful attempt at the trash can. Then ask: *When it comes to throwing paper wads into the trash can, would you say that I am a* **failure** *or a success?* Encourage students to respond. Then say: *Every one of my attempts to make the shot was a* **failure**. Point out that **failure** and "success" are opposites. If you wish, have volunteers attempt to make the shots. After each shot, ask: *Was your attempt a success or a* **failure**? Then have students complete the Day 4 activities on page 88. You may want to do the first one as a group.

DAY 5

Have students complete page 89. Call on students to read aloud their answers to the writing activity.

Day 1 **attempt**

1. How would you complete this sentence? Say it aloud to a partner.

When I attempt something new, I _____ .

2. What might each one *attempt* to do? Draw lines to show your answers.

a. A good skater might attempt   to win a race.

b. Someone who likes to write might attempt   to swim the length of the pool.

c. A good swimmer might attempt   to write a book.

d. A fast runner might attempt   to skate backward.

3. List three things you would like to *attempt*.

a. _____

b. _____

c. _____

Day 2 **attempt**

1. How would you complete this sentence? Say it aloud to a partner.

My first attempt to _____ turned out _____ .

2. In which sentence could *attempt* <u>not</u> replace the underlined word? Circle your answer.

a. After just one <u>try</u>, Carlo broke the piñata.

b. Gillian made a final <u>effort</u> to help her team win.

c. I took the <u>chance</u> to catch up on my homework.

d. It was our first <u>shot</u> at making ice cream.

3. Which of these things are examples of *attempts*? Circle your answers.

a. a change of plans   c. a splinter in your finger

b. a swing at the ball   d. a guess at the right answer

Name _____

Day 3 fail

1. How would you complete this sentence? Say it aloud to a partner.

I think I might fail if I tried to _____.

2. Which phrase best completes this sentence? Circle your answer.

Jason failed to finish his paper because _____.

   a. he wasn't neat

   b. he misspelled some words

   c. he ran out of time

   d. he wrote it too quickly

3. Complete each sentence by writing the word *fail*.

   a. If you lose, you _____ to win.

   b. If you forget, you _____ to remember.

   c. If you miss something, you _____ to notice it.

I don't plan on **failing** the spelling test!

Day 4 failure

1. How would you complete this sentence? Say it aloud to a partner.

It was a failure the first time I attempted to _____.

2. Which of the following are examples of *failure*? Circle your answers.

   a. a chair that breaks

   b. a TV that turns on

   c. a pie that tastes good

   d. a plant that does not grow

3. Tell about a time when you failed. What did you learn from your *failure*?

_____

_____

_____

Daily Academic Vocabulary

Day 5 **attempt • fail • failure**

Fill in the bubble next to the correct answer.

1. If you *attempt* to win a race, you _____.

    Ⓐ prove you can run faster than anyone

    Ⓑ watch to see who will win

    Ⓒ know you will win

    Ⓓ try to be the first one to finish

2. Which sentence could you complete with the word *attempt*?

    Ⓕ Zoe's report card was an _____ to her parents.

    Ⓖ This is Matt's latest _____ to invent a better pencil.

    Ⓗ Ellen used the party as the _____ for a new story.

    Ⓙ Eddie blamed his _____ on being tired.

3. Which of these things could cause a picnic to *fail*?

    Ⓐ happy people

    Ⓑ good food

    Ⓒ heavy rain

    Ⓓ a gentle breeze

4. If someone is a *failure* at hide and seek, they probably _____.

    Ⓕ hide too well

    Ⓖ find their friends too fast

    Ⓗ count too fast

    Ⓙ can't think of good places to hide

Writing Tell about something you hope you will never *fail* in. Be sure to use the word *fail* in your writing.

_____

_____

_____

question • inquire • inquiry

Use the transparency for week 21 and the suggestions on page 6 to introduce the words for each day.

DAY 1

question
(noun) Something asked in order to get an answer or find out something. *April asked a question about what parrots eat.*

Ask these **questions** without waiting for responses: *What day is today? What time is it?* Then say: *I just asked two questions. When we ask questions, we are looking for answers. I am going to ask each question again, and I want you all to answer out loud.* Ask the two **questions**, pausing for a response. Then ask students to give examples of **questions**. Have students complete the Day 1 activities on page 91. You may want to do the first one as a group.

DAY 2

question
(verb) To ask questions of someone or about something. *Mr. Spears questioned the students about what they were reading.*

Say: *When you question someone, you ask him or her questions. What might I ask if I question you about your homework?* Then say: *You can also question as you read. If you are reading a book about penguins, what are some questions you might ask in your head?* Then have students complete the Day 2 activities on page 91. You may want to do the first one as a group.

DAY 3

inquire
(verb) To ask about someone or something. *Augie inquired about his grade on the test.*

inquiry
(noun) A question or request for information. *The principal answered an inquiry about after-school activities.*

Ask several students how they are feeling today. Then say: *I just inquired about your health. When I inquire about your health, I ask how you feel.* Explain that **inquire** means about the same thing as "ask," but **inquire** cannot be used in all the same places as "ask." Ask: *What sorts of things might someone inquire about our school?* (e.g., number of students; what is for lunch) Say: *When you inquire, you make an inquiry. What is an inquiry you might make at a library? At a museum? In a store?* Then have students complete the Day 3 activities on page 92. You may want to do the first one as a group.

DAY 4

inquiry
(noun) A study done to find answers to something. *The school officials conducted an inquiry into attendance problems.*

Say: *Yesterday we learned that inquiry means a request for information. It can also be a study made to find out specific information. It is often used in the phrase "official inquiry."* Who do you think makes official **inquiries**? (e.g., school official; law enforcement) Then say: *There are also scientific inquiries. What might those inquiries investigate?* Then have students complete the Day 4 activities on page 92. You may want to do the first one as a group.

DAY 5

Have students complete page 93. Call on students to read aloud their answers to the writing activity.

Daily Academic Vocabulary

Day 1 question

1. How would you complete this sentence? Say it aloud to a partner.

I like to ask questions when _____.

2. Which of the following sentences are *questions?* Circle your answers.

   a. How many people live in Oklahoma?

   b. Vermont became a state in 1791.

   c. California has the largest population of any state.

   d. When did Alaska become a state?

**3. Rearrange the words in this sentence to turn it into a *question.*
Write the *question* on the lines.**

We are supposed to answer the question on the board.

_____

_____

Day 2 question

1. How would you complete this sentence? Say it aloud to a partner.

After reading, our teacher will question us about _____.

**2. In which of these sentences is the word *question* <u>not</u> used correctly?
Circle your answer.**

   a. The students question the teacher about the project.

   b. Scientists question the causes of natural events.

   c. The reporter questioned the mayor about the plans for a new park.

   d. The group started a question into the cost of new books.

3. What do people do when they *question* someone? Circle your answer.

   a. They make guesses.

   b. They try to find out what the person knows.

   c. They tell someone.

   d. They don't care about the answers.

Name_____

Daily Academic Vocabulary

Day 3 inquire • inquiry

1. How would you complete these sentences? Say them aloud to a partner.

Something I might inquire about at a restaurant is _____.

For help with homework, I make an inquiry of _____.

2. In which sentence can *inquire* <u>not</u> take the place of "ask"? Circle your answer.

a. We called the train station to <u>ask</u> if the train had arrived.

b. When I see Grandma's friends, they always <u>ask</u> about her.

c. Damon hoped the teacher would <u>ask</u> him about snakes.

d. The principal stopped to <u>ask</u> why we were not in our classroom.

3. In which sentence could *inquiry* take the place of the word "question"? Circle your answer.

a. Maya had a <u>question</u> about the poem.

b. The letter came in answer to our <u>question</u>.

c. Our teacher answers every <u>question</u> we ask.

d. The first <u>question</u> on the test was the hardest.

Day 4 inquiry

1. How would you complete this sentence? Say it aloud to a partner.

I would like to make an inquiry into _____.

2. Which phrase best completes this sentence? Circle your answer.

A scientific inquiry found that _____.

a. Pluto was not a planet

b. country is the most popular music

c. there are many bicycles in China

d. Ramona Quimby is an interesting character

An **inquiry** would prove that parrots are the best birds!

3. Which of these words has about the same meaning as *inquiry*? Circle your answer.

a. trace   c. study

b. opinion   d. subject

Daily Academic Vocabulary

Day 5 **question • inquire • inquiry**

Fill in the bubble next to the correct answer.

1. Which sentence does not tell about a *question*?

Ⓐ It ends with a question mark.

Ⓑ It might start with "who," "what," "where," "when," "why," or "how."

Ⓒ You make a statement.

Ⓓ You ask one to find out something.

2. Which of these words does not mean about the same thing as *question*?

Ⓕ inquire

Ⓖ ask

Ⓗ understand

Ⓙ wonder

3. Which sentence uses the word *inquire* correctly?

Ⓐ The students wanted to inquire new library books.

Ⓑ You can inquire about overdue book fines at the front desk.

Ⓒ Most libraries inquire that people speak softly.

Ⓓ I will inquire Hilary to come with me to the library.

4. Which of these is a good subject for an official *inquiry*?

Ⓕ how schools spend their money

Ⓖ how many games each student owns

Ⓗ how many kids like ice cream

Ⓙ what kids' favorite toys are

Writing Think of a book character. What would you ask if you could *question* that character? Use one of this week's words in your writing.

_____

_____

_____

contain • consist • include

Use the transparency for week 22 and the suggestions on page 6 to introduce the words for each day.

DAY 1

contain
(verb) To hold or have within itself. *This closet **contains** the art supplies.*

Display a box of crayons. Say: *This box **contains** crayons.* Open a cupboard or a closet. Ask: *What does this cupboard (or closet) **contain**?* Gesture toward the bookshelves. Ask: *What do the bookshelves **contain**?* Encourage students to use the word **contain** in their responses. Then have students complete the Day 1 activities on page 95. You may want to do the first one as a group.

DAY 2

contain
(verb) To be made up of things. *Some people cannot eat foods that **contain** nuts.*

Display a box of snacks that has a contents label. Say: *These snacks **contain**…* and start reading out the ingredients. Ask: *What does your favorite cookie **contain**?* Then display a book of short stories or poems. Say: *This book **contains** many short stories (or poems). The stories (or poems) make up the book.* Then have students complete the Day 2 activities on page 95. You may want to do the first one as a group.

DAY 3

consist
(verb) To be made up of; contain. *Your homework today **consists** of math problems and a punctuation worksheet.*

Tell students that we often use the phrase "**consists** of." Ask: *What does a week **consist** of?* (7 days) *What does a year **consist** of?* (365 days or 12 months) *What does (or did) your lunch **consist** of?* Mention that although **consist** and "contain" have similar meanings, they can't always be used interchangeably. Say: *We would not say that a week contains 7 days or that a day contains 24 hours.* Then have students complete the Day 3 activities on page 96. You may want to do the first one as a group.

DAY 4

include
(verb) To have or contain as part of the whole. *Our school population **includes** teachers, students, and staff.*

Show students a reading textbook. Say: *This book **includes** many stories. The stories are part of the whole thing, which is the book. A family is a whole thing that **includes** people, and perhaps pets, as a part of it.* Ask: *What does your family **include**?* Allow several students to respond. Encourage them to use the word **include** in their responses. Then have students complete the Day 4 activities on page 96. You may want to do the first one as a group.

DAY 5

Have students complete page 97. Call on students to read aloud their answers to the writing activity.

Name _____

Day 1 contain

1. How would you complete this sentence? Say it aloud to a partner.

My school bag contains _____.

**2. Match each thing named on the left with what it *contains*.
Draw lines to show your answers.**

a. The ocean contains   articles and pictures.

b. A dictionary contains   people traveling somewhere.

c. A magazine contains   words and their meanings.

d. An airplane contains   different kinds of sea animals.

**3. What could a big box *contain*? Write a sentence to answer the question.
Be sure to include the word *contain*.**

_____

_____

Day 2 contain

1. How would you complete this sentence? Say it aloud to a partner.

My favorite meal contains _____.

2. What two things do both of these snacks *contain*? Circle your answer.

Banana Berry Smoothie   Fruit Yogurt Salad
    fresh berries   fresh berries
    yogurt   melon
    banana   yogurt

a. fresh berries and banana   c. fresh berries and melon

b. yogurt and banana   d. fresh berries and yogurt

3. In which sentence is the word *contain* used correctly? Circle your answer.

a. Contain your name on the test.   c. The speech contains many jokes.

b. A song contains the band.   d. Carrots contain in a salad.

Day 3 consist

1. How would you complete this sentence? Say it aloud to a partner.

My favorite dessert consists of these ingredients: _____.

2. What does each thing *consist* of? Draw lines to show your answers.

a. papier-mâché   animals, acrobats, clowns

b. a birthday party   cake, friends, presents

c. a circus   common interests, caring, shared times

d. a friendship   strips of paper, paste

3. Which sentence uses the word *consist* correctly? Circle your answer.

a. A healthy meal consists of more than one food group.

b. My crayon box does not consist of a red crayon.

c. If you consist, I will go with you to the movies.

d. How many marbles does the jar consist of?

Day 4 include

1. How would you complete this sentence? Say it aloud to a partner.

My whole family includes _____.

**2. Match each group with the names of things *included* in that group.
Draw lines to show your answers.**

a. names of states   title, table of contents, index, glossary

b. kinds of trees   oceans, rivers, lakes, ponds

c. parts of a book   oak, maple, pine, redwood

d. bodies of water   Maine, Florida, Texas, Oregon

**3. In which animal group would you *include* lizards and snakes?
Circle your answer.**

a. insects   c. fish

b. birds   d. reptiles

Day 5 **contain • consist • include**

Fill in the bubble next to the correct answer.

1. What is someone's school desk <u>not</u> likely to *contain*?

   Ⓐ books

   Ⓑ crayons

   Ⓒ paper

   Ⓓ a dog

2. Which of these foods does <u>not</u> *contain* fruit?

   Ⓕ grape juice

   Ⓖ strawberry ice cream

   Ⓗ vegetable soup

   Ⓙ blueberry yogurt

3. In which sentence could the phrase "*consists* of" take the place of "contains"?

   Ⓐ A good book <u>contains</u> interesting characters and an exciting plot.

   Ⓑ The drawer <u>contains</u> socks.

   Ⓒ The aquarium <u>contains</u> three fish.

   Ⓓ That paragraph <u>contains</u> many errors.

4. If you are included in a group, you _____.

   Ⓕ are by yourself

   Ⓖ must lead the others

   Ⓗ must do what they say

   Ⓙ are a member of the group

Writing Tell what books you would *include* in a list of your three favorite books. Be sure to use the word *include* in your writing.

_____

_____

_____

Daily Academic Vocabulary

produce • productive • product

Use the transparency for week 23 and the suggestions on page 6 to introduce the words for each day.

DAY 1	**produce** *(verb)* To build or make. *The sun **produces** heat and light.*	Say: *Factories **produce** things such as cars, paper, and food.* Ask: *What do chickens **produce**?* (meat; eggs) *What do trees **produce**?* (nuts; leaves; carbon dioxide) *What do people **produce**?* (inventions; buildings; pollution; more people) Then ask: *What other places or animals **produce** things we need?* Have students respond using the sentence starter, "___ **produce(s)** ___." Then have students complete the Day 1 activities on page 99. You may want to do the first one as a group.
DAY 2	**productive** *(adj.)* Producing large amounts. *Robertson's apple orchard is the most **productive** orchard in the county.*	Describe this scenario for students: *Let's pretend you are working with a partner to solve some math problems, and I say, "You are being extremely **productive**!" Would I mean that you were goofing around and not working? What would I mean?* Guide students to state that being **productive** means getting a lot done or producing a lot. Ask: *Who would like to tell about a time this week when you felt **productive**?* Then have students complete the Day 2 activities on page 99. You may want to do the first one as a group.
DAY 3	**product** *(noun)* Something that is made. *Cheese and yogurt are dairy **products**.*	Point out that **products** are things that are produced or made. Ask: *What sorts of things are **products**? Look around the room. What things are the **product** of students? What things are the **product** of a teacher? Of a paper company?* Invite students to name examples of **products**, using the word **product** in their responses. Finally, have students complete the Day 3 activities on page 100. You may want to do the first one as a group.
DAY 4	**product** *(noun)* A result that follows from something else. *Marcie's good grades were the **product** of hard work.*	Explain that **product** can also refer to something that comes about as a result of something else. Say: *A **product** of studying might be success or good grades.* Ask: *What might be a **product** of hurrying or being careless?* (e.g., an accident; a mistake) Say: ***Products** can be good or bad.* Then have students complete the Day 4 activities on page 100. You may want to do the first one as a group.
DAY 5		Have students complete page 101. Call on students to read aloud their answers to the writing activity.

Daily Academic Vocabulary

Day 1 produce

1. How would you complete this sentence? Say it aloud to a partner.

I can use _____ to produce a _____.

2. In which sentence can the word *produce* take the place of "make"? Circle your answer.

a. Stephanie tells jokes to <u>make</u> people laugh.

b. American factories <u>make</u> millions of cars every year.

c. Some kids <u>make</u> money by doing jobs for their parents.

d. Strawberries <u>make</u> Tina break out in hives.

3. What does each of the things listed at the left *produce*? Draw lines to show your answers.

a. A whistle produces   a cool breeze.

b. A dairy produces   heat and light.

c. A campfire produces   milk, cheese, and ice cream.

d. A fan produces   a loud blast of sound.

Day 2 productive

1. How would you complete this sentence? Say it aloud to a partner.

I feel most productive when _____.

2. Which sentence describes a person who is *productive*? Circle your answer.

a. Felicia daydreamed about what she would do if she won the big prize.

b. Taylor meant to take her dog for a walk on Saturday.

c. Romero ate a sandwich for lunch every day this week.

d. Tran read three books and completed a book report on each one.

3. Which sentence can be completed with the word *productive*? Circle your answer.

a. Elias made _____ cookies for everyone on his birthday.

b. Penny _____ every word correctly on the spelling test.

c. Bailey's group stayed with the task and was the most _____.

d. Kayla said that our team had the best _____.

Day 3 | product

1. How would you complete this sentence? Say it aloud to a partner.

One product that makes my life easier is _____.

2. Which of the following is <u>not</u> a *product*? Circle your answer.

    a. apple juice   c. shoes

    b. air   d. shampoo

3. In which sentence is the word *product* used correctly? Circle your answer.

    a. The hotel was a smaller product of a famous castle in Spain.

    b. The farm stand sells berries and products made from berries.

    c. Passing out the workbooks is a regular classroom product.

    d. Silly poems can sometimes be the products of stories.

Day 4 | product

1. How would you complete this sentence? Say it aloud to a partner.

Having success at something is the product of _____.

2. Which phrase best completes this sentence? Circle your answer.

The class's science project was the product of _____.

    a. the principal's announcement   c. the students' teamwork

    b. dirt, seeds, and jars   d. first prize in the contest

3. In which sentence could the word *product* take the place of "result"? Circle your answer.

    a. The argument was the <u>result</u> of a misunderstanding.

    b. As a <u>result</u> of all the rain, the grass grew very fast.

    c. The test <u>result</u> showed that the dog was sick.

    d. We put a white flower in blue water and watched the <u>result</u>.

Daily Academic Vocabulary

Day 5 **produce • productive**

Fill in the bubble next to the correct answer.

1. Which sentence does <u>not</u> use the word *produce* correctly?

Ⓒ Bells produce a bright, happy sound.

Ⓓ Our class will produce its own newspaper.

Ⓔ Some scientists produce that the Earth is getting warmer.

Ⓕ Power plants produce electricity.

2. A *productive* vegetable garden might _____.

Ⓕ have a fence around it

Ⓖ have a lot of weeds

Ⓗ not need any care

Ⓘ give a lot of tomatoes

3. Which of the following is the best definition for *product*?

Ⓒ something made in a kitchen

Ⓓ something made up of different things

Ⓔ something made by people or made in nature

Ⓕ something that occurs in nature

My favorite **product** is parrot food!

4. Winning the race was the *product* of _____.

Ⓕ good luck

Ⓖ months of training

Ⓗ good shoes

Ⓘ good weather for running

Writing Tell about a favorite *product* that your family buys and uses. Be sure to use the word *product* in your writing.

_____

_____

_____

cause • effect • effective

Use the transparency for week 24 and the suggestions on page 6 to introduce the words for each day.

DAY 1

cause
(noun) The reason why something happens. *Warm temperatures were the cause of the snowman melting.*

Place a feather or tissue on an empty table where students can see. Then blow on it to make it move across the table. Ask: *What just happened?* Then ask: *What was the cause of the movement?* Help students recognize that blowing on the feather (or tissue) was the **cause**. Say: *The cause is what makes something happen. It can be an action or an event. It can be a feeling or something someone says.* Explore the **causes** of things that have happened in the classroom recently. (e.g., a reward; an argument; a fall) Then have students complete the Day 1 activities on page 103. You may want to do the first one as a group.

DAY 2

cause
(verb) To make something happen. *A patch of ice caused the car to skid.*

Blow the feather or tissue across the table. **Cause** it to fall off the table. Say: *I just caused the feather (or tissue) to fall.* Explain that **cause** can be both a noun and a verb. Then have students complete the Day 2 activities on page 103. You may want to do the first one as a group.

DAY 3

effect
(noun) Something produced by a cause. *The forest fire was the effect of lightning striking several trees.*

Explain that "cause" and **effect** go together. Say: *The cause is the reason, or what makes something happen. The effect is what happens.* Blow the feather or tissue across the table again until it falls off. Say: *Blowing on the feather (or tissue) is the cause. The feather (or tissue) moving and falling off the table is the effect.* Read the sample sentence and have students identify the cause and the **effect**. Then have students complete the Day 3 activities on page 104. You may want to do the first one as a group.

DAY 4

effective
(adj.) Able to bring about a result. *The book fair was effective in raising money for new computers.*

Place the feather (or tissue) on the table once again. Explain that something is **effective** if it brings about the desired effect. First, try to fan it across the table with your hand. Then blow it across the table again. Ask: *Which method was more effective at moving the feather (or tissue)—fanning it or blowing on it?* Ask: *What things are effective in helping you do your homework?* (e.g., computer; school books; pencil; paper) Then have students complete the Day 4 activities on page 104. You may want to do the first one as a group.

DAY 5

Have students complete page 105. Call on students to read aloud their answers to the writing activity.

Name_____

Day 1 cause

1. How would you complete this sentence? Say it aloud to a partner.

_____ is always a cause for laughter.

2. Which of the following could be the *cause* of a fall? Circle your answers.

    a. a bumpy sidewalk   c. a broken arm

    b. a scraped knee   d. a wet and slippery floor

3. Which phrase best completes this sentence? Circle your answer.

The cause of the many large flowers was _____.

    a. the gardener   c. a month without rain

    b. picking the flowers   d. water, sunlight, and good soil

Day 2 cause

1. How would you complete this sentence? Say it aloud to a partner.

Thinking about lunch causes me to _____.

2. Which of these phrases could <u>not</u> complete this sentence? Circle your answer.

A giant snowstorm caused _____.

    a. schools to be closed   c. flowers to bloom

    b. cars to get stuck   d. people to stay at home

3. Which of these things might *cause* you to catch a cold? Circle your answer.

    a. sneezing

    b. eating good food

    c. being near someone who has a cold

    d. having a runny nose

Day 3 effect

1. How would you complete this sentence? Say it aloud to a partner.

One effect of reading is _____.

**2. Match the causes at the left with the *effects* at the right.
Draw lines to show your answers.**

Cause	Effect
a. You eat too much food.	You stay home from school.
b. You get sick.	You get a blister on your foot.
c. A mosquito bites your arm.	You get an itchy bump.
d. You wear shoes that don't fit.	You get a stomachache.

**3. Which of these things are *effects* of eating well and getting exercise?
Circle your answers.**

a. You stay healthy.   c. You spend more time watching TV.

b. You get sick more often.   d. Your body feels good.

Day 4 effective

1. How would you complete this sentence? Say it aloud to a partner.

One effective way to study spelling words is _____.

2. Which one best describes a plan that is *effective*? Circle your answer.

a. It is hard to understand.   c. It is not original.

b. It cannot be done.   d. It works.

3. Which sentence does <u>not</u> use the word *effective* correctly? Circle your answer.

a. E-mail is an effective way to stay in touch with friends.

b. Plain soap was not effective in removing the stain.

c. Every student had an effective copy of the worksheet.

d. The fan was effective in cooling the room.

Day 5 cause • effect • effective

Fill in the bubble next to the correct answer.

1. Which sentence uses the word *cause* correctly?

Ⓐ Missing the bus was the cause of Karin's oversleeping.

Ⓑ Jamie's smile was the cause of hearing a joke.

Ⓒ A flat tire was the cause of us missing soccer practice.

Ⓓ Shade in the summer was one cause of planting trees.

2. In which sentence could *causes* take the place of the underlined word?

Ⓕ The moon <u>changes</u> its appearance a little each night.

Ⓖ The Earth's rotation <u>makes</u> day and night.

Ⓗ Tad told us the <u>reasons</u> why he liked the book.

Ⓙ Being in a bad mood never <u>excuses</u> being rude.

3. The trash on the beach was the *effect* of _____.

Ⓐ people playing in the sand

Ⓑ a dirty beach

Ⓒ people not using trash cans

Ⓓ animals getting sick

4. Which word has about the same meaning as *effective*?

Ⓕ cause

Ⓖ scary

Ⓗ careless

Ⓙ useful

Writing   Think about your favorite song. What *effect* does it have on you? Why does it *cause* this *effect*? Use the words *cause* and *effect* in your writing.

_____

_____

_____

Daily Academic Vocabulary

handle • control

Use the transparency for week 25 and the suggestions on page 6 to introduce the words for each day.

DAY 1

handle
(verb) To touch or hold with the hands. *Be gentle when you* **handle** *the kitten.*

Show students a coffee cup and point to the handle. Say: *You know the name of this part of the cup. It's called the handle.* **Handle** *can also be a verb, something you do. If this cup had hot coffee in it, I would* **handle** *it, or hold it, with care.* Then have them name things in the room that they **handle**. (e.g., books; math manipulatives; clay) Finally, have students complete the Day 1 activities on page 107. You may want to do the first one as a group.

DAY 2

handle
(verb) To take care of a problem or situation; to deal with. *Ms. Ruiz will* **handle** *putting the books on the shelves.*

Call attention to some classroom housekeeping task that needs doing. (e.g., straightening books on a table) Call on a student and ask: *Can you* **handle** *that for me later on?* When the student has responded, explain that when people say they can **handle** something, it means they can take care of it; they can do it. Ask: *When have you* **handled** *a problem or task at school? At home?* Then have students complete the Day 2 activities on page 107. You may want to do the first one as a group.

DAY 3

control
(verb) To make someone or something do what you want; to direct. *The principal* **controls** *the school schedule.*

Say: *When you* **control** *someone, you make him or her do what you want. Cinderella's stepmother* **controlled** *Cinderella by giving her chores and not letting her go to the ball. You can also* **control** *things.* Show students the light switch. Say: *This device* **controls** *the lights in the room.* Ask: *What can* **control** *a TV?* (remote) *What* **controls** *a car?* (driver; steering wheel) Then have students complete the Day 3 activities on page 108. You may want to do the first one as a group.

DAY 4

control
(noun) Power over something. *The principal has* **control** *over the school schedule.*

Say: **Control** *is also the power that you have over something. For example, because I am the teacher, I have* **control** *over this classroom. I decide what we will do.* Ask: *What do you have* **control** *over?* (e.g., their actions; words) Encourage students to use the word **control** in their answers. Then have students complete the Day 4 activities on page 108. You may want to do the first one as a group.

DAY 5

Have students complete page 109. Call on students to read aloud their answers to the writing activity.

Daily
Academic
Vocabulary

Day 1 handle

1. How would you complete this sentence? Say it aloud to a partner.

I am always very careful when I handle _____.

2. Which of these might be in a box with _"handle with care"_ written on it? Circle your answers.

a. a glass vase
c. a pair of shoes
b. a pillow
d. a watch

3. Which phrase best completes this sentence? Circle your answer.

Before you handle food, you should _____.

a. take off your oven mitts
b. be sure the food is clean
c. take it out of the refrigerator
d. make sure your hands are clean

Day 2 handle

1. How would you complete this sentence? Say it aloud to a partner.

When _____ asked me to _____, I knew I could handle it.

2. In which sentence can the underlined words not be replaced by _handle?_ Circle your answer.

a. Ms. Dowd will <u>take charge of</u> all the arrangements for the party.
b. Barry was sure that he could <u>be successful in</u> the job.
c. Please <u>turn in</u> your test paper when you have finished.
d. The whole family trusted Dad to <u>take care of</u> everything.

3. Which of these jobs do you think you could _handle?_ Circle your answers.

a. being a doctor
c. feeding a pet
b. picking flowers
d. building a house

I can **handle** anything!

Name_____

Daily Academic Vocabulary

Day 3 | control

1. How would you complete this sentence? Say it aloud to a partner.

I wish I had a device to control _____.

2. Which phrase best completes this sentence? Circle your answer.

Brianna tried to control the book club by _____.

a. letting everyone talk at once   c. never coming to meetings

b. making up lots of rules   d. asking the teacher questions

3. Which of these things do people *control*? Circle your answers.

a. what they choose to buy at the store

b. when it will rain

c. what they do in their free time

d. when the sun comes up

Day 4 | control

1. How would you complete this sentence? Say it aloud to a partner.

My parents have control over _____.

2. Match each person with what he or she takes *control* of. Draw lines to show your answers.

a. A pilot   takes control of fires.

b. A firefighter   has control over the players.

c. A coach   takes control of a group.

d. A leader   has control over a plane.

3. List three things you have *control* over.

a. _____

b. _____

c. _____

Name_____

Day 5 **handle • control**

Fill in the bubble next to the correct answer.

1. Which sentence uses the word *handle* correctly?

Ⓐ The teacher asked Jake to handle him the report.

Ⓑ Monica doesn't like to handle anything that's wet and slimy.

Ⓒ Everyone handled their tickets to the man at the door.

Ⓓ It's Shandra's turn to handle out the worksheets.

2. Which statement tells what it means to *handle* a problem?

Ⓕ You hand it off to someone else.

Ⓖ You make trouble.

Ⓗ You take care of things.

Ⓙ You write down everything that happens.

3. The bus driver *controls* the bus by _____.

Ⓐ sitting in front

Ⓑ owning it

Ⓒ parking it in front of the school

Ⓓ steering it and using the brakes

4. Which sentence is <u>not</u> true?

Ⓕ A principal has control over how a school is run.

Ⓖ Teachers have control over what their students do in class.

Ⓗ A librarian has control over what is written in books.

Ⓙ Parents can have some control over what their children watch on TV.

Writing What is the hardest task you have *handled?* Tell what you did to *handle* it. Be sure to use the word *handle* in your sentence.

_____

_____

_____

recall • recount
memorize • recite

Use the transparency for week 26 and the suggestions on page 6 to introduce the words for each day.

DAY 1

recall
(verb) To remember something. *Mom couldn't* **recall** *the name of the bookstore.*

Explain that **recall** has the same meaning as "remember." Say: *When you* **recall** *something, you call it back out of your memory. That's the same thing you do when you remember.* Have students use "remember" in sentences. Repeat each sentence, substituting **recall** for "remember." Then have students complete the Day 1 activities on page 111. You may want to do the first one as a group.

DAY 2

recount
(verb) To tell about something that happened. *The guest speaker will* **recount** *his adventures in Africa.*

Have students tell what they do when they retell a story. Say: *When you* **recount** *something that happened, it's a lot like retelling a story. You tell the whole sequence of events.* Recall a recent shared class experience, and ask a student to **recount** it. Then say: *(Student's name) just* **recounted** *an experience we all shared.* Finally, have students complete the Day 2 activities on page 111. You may want to do the first one as a group.

DAY 3

memorize
(verb) To learn something by heart. *Jana has* **memorized** *all her friends' phone numbers.*

recite
(verb) To say aloud something you have memorized. *Husna can* **recite** *all fifty state capitals.*

Tell students that you are going to **recite** a poem or quotation. After doing so, say: *I can* **recite** *that poem (or quotation) because I* **memorized** *it. I don't have to read it.* Say: ***Memorize*** *and "remember" are both related to "memory," but they don't mean exactly the same thing. You can remember a book in that you know the characters and what happens, but that doesn't mean you have* **memorized** *it. If you* **memorize** *something that is written, you can* **recite** *it, or repeat every word of it.* Ask: *Can any of you* **recite** *something you have memorized?* Then have students complete the Day 3 activities on page 112. You may want to do the first one as a group.

DAY 4

recite
(verb) To list or tell about in detail. *James* **recited** *a long list of people who came to his party.*

Say: ***Recite*** *can also describe what people do when they tell you a long list of things or tell a story that includes every detail. For example, last night I (***recite*** *a list of things you did).* Ask: *What are some things you can* **recite** *that are not things you have memorized?* (e.g., class rules, chores, names of relatives) Have students complete the Day 4 activities on page 112. You may want to do the first one as a group.

DAY 5

Have students complete page 113. Call on students to read aloud their answers to the writing activity.

Name _____

Day 1   recall

1. How would you complete this sentence? Say it aloud to a partner.

I recall that we learned about _____ yesterday.

2. In which sentence can you not use *recall* in place of "remember"? Circle your answer.

     a. Caitlin couldn't remember the words to the song.

     b. It's fun to remember the good times we had on vacation.

     c. Did you remember to turn out the light?

     d. I think I know that girl, but I can't remember her name.

3. What can you *recall* about the last book you read? Write three things about it.

     a. _____

     b. _____

     c. _____

Day 2   recount

1. How would you complete this sentence? Say it aloud to a partner.

I like to recount the time I _____.

2. Which of the following describes *recounting* something? Circle your answers.

     a. telling the story of something that happened to you

     b. remembering what was on a lost shopping list

     c. reciting the words to a favorite song

     d. telling your family about your day at school

3. Which sentence can you complete with the word *recount*? Circle your answer.

     a. Our teacher can _____ the names of all her students.

     b. Bao couldn't _____ where he'd left his jacket.

     c. Joni tries to _____ a new poem every week.

     d. Alison's report will _____ the story of Christopher Columbus.

Day 3 **memorize • recite**

1. **How would you complete these sentences? Say them aloud to a partner.**

    I have memorized a _____.

    I will recite it to _____.

2. **Which of these things would someone be likely to** *memorize?*
   Circle your answers.

    a. lines from a play

    b. a whole chapter from a book

    c. the words to a song

    d. parts of the phone book

3. **Write the first two lines of a song or poem that you have** *memorized*
   and can recite.

   _____

   _____

   _____

Day 4 **recite**

1. **How would you complete this sentence? Say it aloud to a partner.**

    A list that I could recite is _____.

2. **Which phrases could complete the sentence? Circle your answers.**

    We listened to Bibi recite _____.

    a. a long list of things she had to do

    b. her bike

    c. the names of all the states

    d. her idea for the project

3. **Which sentence could <u>not</u> be completed with the word** *recite?*
   Circle your answer.

    a. Kirby likes to _____ facts about baseball players.

    b. Sarah likes to _____ all the places she went on vacation.

    c. Serena likes to _____ the names of all her pets.

    d. Fred likes to _____ copying animal sounds.

Day 5 recall • recount • memorize • recite

Fill in the bubble next to the correct answer.

1. When you *recall* a detail, you _____.

Ⓐ rewrite it

Ⓑ take it out of your story

Ⓒ remember it

Ⓓ decide if it's important or not

2. If you *recount* an adventure, you _____.

Ⓕ tell about it

Ⓖ make it up in your head

Ⓗ change your story about it

Ⓙ remember something you have read

3. Which sentence could you complete with the word *memorize*?

Ⓐ Fiona was eager to _____ the new movie.

Ⓑ Mom helped Audra _____ her part in the play.

Ⓒ Carlo couldn't _____ how he spent his birthday money.

Ⓓ We listened to Evan _____ his trumpet.

4. In which sentence is the word *recite* <u>not</u> used correctly?

Ⓕ Danielle can recite the names of all twelve of her cousins.

Ⓖ Angela taught her little sister to recite the alphabet.

Ⓗ Iman has watched the movie so often he can recite parts of it.

Ⓙ Desmond needs to recite his dance for the school show.

Writing Explain why you might need to *memorize* something. Be sure to use the word *memorize* in your writing.

_____

_____

_____

CUMULATIVE REVIEW
WORDS FROM WEEKS 19–26

attempt
cause
consider
consist
contain
control
decide
decision
effect
effective
fail
failure
handle
include
inquire
inquiry
memorize
produce
product
productive
question
recall
recite
recount

Days 1–4

Each day's activity is a cloze paragraph that students complete with words or forms of words that they have learned in weeks 19–26. Before students begin, pronounce each word in the box on the student page, have students repeat each word, and then review each word's meaning(s). **Other ways to review the words:**

- Start a sentence containing one of the words and have students finish the sentence orally. For example:

    *One **cause** of pollution is…*
    *I hope I will not be a **failure** in…*

- Provide students with a definition and ask them to supply the word that fits it.

- Ask questions that require students to know the meaning of each word. For example:

    *What is an **effective** way to learn a new word?*
    *What can you **recall** about the last book you read?*

- Have students use each word in a sentence.

Day 5

Start by reviewing the four words not practiced on Days 1–4: **decision, effect, handle, inquire**. Write the words on the board and have students repeat them after you. Provide a sentence for one of the words. Ask students to think of their own sentence and share it with a partner. Call on several students to share their sentences. Follow the same procedure for the remaining words. Then have students complete the code-breaker activity.

Extension Ideas

Use any of the following activities to help integrate the vocabulary words into other content areas:

- Help students find or name several **products** that are **produced** in your community.

- Have students discuss why understanding **cause** and **effect** is important when you are reading. Examine the role of **cause** and **effect** in a book or story.

- Discuss with students the sorts of things that people **memorize**. Then ask volunteers to **recite** something they have **memorized**, or assign the class to **memorize** something.

- Have students explain the **effect** of the Earth circling the sun each year. Demonstrate what happens with a globe and a flashlight.

Daily
Academic
Vocabulary

| attempted | consisted | decide | fail | produced |
| consider | control | effective | memorize | recite |

Day 1

Fill in the blanks with words from the word box.

Many people _____ Thomas Edison to be the

inventor of the light bulb. He wasn't. He invented the first light bulb

that _____ light safely. This invention provided an

_____ way to light homes and businesses without using

candles or gas. He also formed an electrical power company to

_____ getting electricity to homes.

Day 2

Fill in the blanks with words from the word box.

Byrne's teacher asked everyone to _____ a poem.

They had a week to learn their poem. Then they had to _____

their poem for the whole class. Byrne couldn't _____ which

poem to choose. His favorite poem _____ of many stanzas.

If he _____ to learn a really long poem, he was afraid he

might _____. He practiced and studied his poem every day.

He was a success!

Daily
Academic
Vocabulary

cause	include	products	recall	failure
contains	inquiry	questions	recount	

Day 3

Fill in the blanks with words from the word box.

It's a good idea to read the labels on food _____.

Reading the label will answer _____ about what the food

_____. Things like nuts can _____ problems

for some people. _____ to read labels might lead to

people eating something they shouldn't.

Day 4

Fill in the blanks with words from the word box.

Suppose someone asked you to _____ to them

what happened at school yesterday. How would you respond to that

_____? What would you say? Would you tell everything

that you could _____, or just the important things? If you

told only the important things, what events would you _____?

Daily
Academic
Vocabulary

Day 5

Crack the Code!

Write one of the words from the word box on the lines beneath each clue.

attempt	decide	failure	inquiry	question
cause	decision	handle	memorize	recall
consider	effect	include	produce	recite
contain	effective	inquire	product	recount
control	fail			

1. When you make up your mind, this is the result.

   ___ ___ ___ ___ ___ ___ ___ ___
        1   2

2. to try to do something

   ___ ___ ___ ___ ___ ___ ___
   3   4

3. what you do when you learn something by heart

   ___ ___ ___ ___ ___ ___ ___ ___
              5

4. what you do when you ask for information

   ___ ___ ___ ___ ___ ___ ___
                          6

5. something caused by something else

   ___ ___ ___ ___ ___ ___
                   7

6. what you make when you ask for information

   ___ ___ ___ ___ ___ ___ ___
       8   9

Now use the numbers under the letters to crack the code. Write the letters
on the lines below. The words will complete this quotation.

Thomas Edison said, "Genius is 1 percent inspiration and 99 percent _____."

___ ___ ___ ___ ___ ___ ___ ___ ___ ___ ___ ___
 4   6   9   2   4   1   9   3   7   1   5   8

term • label

Use the transparency for week 28 and the suggestions on page 6 to introduce the words for each day.

DAY 1

term
(noun) A word having a specific meaning. *The **terms** "note" and "rest" have special meanings in music.*

Write the words "main idea," "plot," "character," and "conclusion" on the board. Ask: *What do these words have in common?* Explain that these words are all literary **terms**. Say: *Each school subject uses **terms**, or special words. What are some **terms** you know that we use in writing?* (paragraph; punctuation; capitalization) *What are some **terms** we use in science?* (experiment; matter; eclipse) Then ask: *What are some other things you can think of that have their own **terms**?* (jobs; sports; hobbies) Then have students complete the Day 1 activities on page 119. You may want to do the first one as a group.

DAY 2

label
(noun) A tag or sticker that is attached to an object and gives useful information. *The **label** on the cereal box tells what is inside.*

(verb) To attach a label to an object. *We will **label** the boxes so we know what is inside.*

Show students different products that have **labels**. Say: *Each of these products has a **label**. Manufacturers **label** products so that people know what they contain.* Explore with students the sorts of things people might **label** and the kinds of information that the **label** might provide. Call on students to complete these sentences: "I would put a **label** on ___. I would use ___ to **label** it." Then have students complete the Day 2 activities on page 119. You may want to do the first one as a group.

DAY 3

label
(noun) A word or phrase that describes someone or something. *The drawing of the sailboat had **labels** that told the name of each part.*

Locate in one of the students' textbooks a picture or diagram that has **labels** and direct students to it. Have students look at the **labels**. Ask: *What information do the **labels** give us?* Discuss why **labels** might be added to an illustration. Then have students complete the Day 3 activities on page 120. You may want to do the first one as a group.

DAY 4

label
(verb) To write the names of parts or items. *We drew a picture of a spider and **labeled** the parts of its body.*

Draw a simple map of the classroom on the board or a chart. Say: *Let's **label** the things I have included in this map of our room.* Invite students to **label** details on your map. Say: *When you **label** something, you help people understand what it is.* Then have students complete the Day 4 activities on page 120. You may want to do the first one as a group.

DAY 5

Have students complete page 121. Call on students to read aloud their answers to the writing activity.

Name_____

Day 1 **term**

1. How would you complete this sentence? Say it aloud to a partner.

"Mouse," "Web site," and _____ are a few computer terms I know.

2. Which group of words are *terms* you know from math? Circle your answer.

    a. noun, verb, adjective   c. download, memory, software

    b. sum, multiply, subtract   d. mammal, habitat, predator

3. Which sentence correctly uses the word *term*? Circle your answer.

    a. A library is a term where you can borrow books.

    b. Fred made a term of the city out of cardboard boxes.

    c. "Nocturnal" is a term that means "active at night."

    d. A star is a term in the night sky.

Day 2 **label**

1. How would you complete these sentences? Say them aloud to a partner.

The label on a food container tells _____.

We label things in our classroom so that _____.

2. Which of these things usually have *labels*? Circle your answers.

    a.   b.   c.   d.

3. Why might you *label* a box or jar? Circle your answer.

    a. so you can close it tightly

    b. so whatever is inside will keep better

    c. so you know what is inside

    d. to make it look nice

Day 3 label

1. How would you complete this sentence? Say it aloud to a partner.

Labels on a diagram of our school would help new students _____.

2. Draw lines to connect the *labels* with the correct parts of the illustration.

Molly Logan
532 Union St.
Barre, VT 05578

    Ms. Wendy Hill
    3700 Cascades Dr.
    Portland, OR 95478

stamp

return address

address

3. Which *labels* might you put on a drawing of a butterfly? Circle your answers.

a. head   c. flipper
b. wing   d. teeth

Day 4 label

1. How would you complete this sentence? Say it aloud to a partner.

If I drew a picture of a tiger, I would label _____.

2. In which sentence is the word *label* used correctly? Circle your answer.

a. The teacher showed us how to label a butterfly out of paper.
b. We will label the room with paper airplanes.
c. For the test, we had to label the parts of a caterpillar.
d. Gina's job is to label the party.

3. Which of these things might you *label*? Circle your answers.

a. places on a map in a book
b. the parts of a letter you write
c. a picture you hang on your wall
d. the parts of an octopus in a drawing

Label me!

Name_____

Day 5 term • label

Fill in the bubble next to the correct answer.

1. Which sentence uses the word *term* correctly?

Ⓐ Friendliness is a term of many dogs, cats, and other pets.

Ⓑ Recycle is a term for making new things from old ones.

Ⓒ Fairness is a term all teachers should have.

Ⓓ A term is a label on a picture.

2. Which of these things would be least likely to have a *label*?

Ⓕ a milk jug

Ⓖ a watermelon

Ⓗ a jar of peanut butter

Ⓙ a box of crackers

3. Why would you put *labels* on a drawing?

Ⓐ to tell what the parts are

Ⓑ to tell how you did it

Ⓒ to tell why you drew it

Ⓓ to give the picture a name

4. If you *labeled* objects in the classroom, you would _____.

Ⓕ tell what everything is made of

Ⓖ put a student's name on every object

Ⓗ put a sign on each object that tells its name

Ⓙ group them by size and color

Writing   Tell why you think *labels* are useful and important. Be sure to use the word *label* in your writing.

_____

_____

_____

conduct • operate • process

Use the transparency for week 29 and the suggestions on page 6 to introduce the words for each day.

DAY 1

conduct
(verb) To manage or direct something. *The museum conducted a study to find out which exhibits people liked best.*

(verb) To lead or guide. *The principal conducts a tour of the school for new students.*

Say: *Let's conduct a survey to find out your favorite season. Who here thinks that spring is the best season? Summer? Fall? Winter?* Record the results on the board. Then say: *We conducted a survey to learn about your favorite seasons.* Then say: *Conduct can also mean "to lead or guide someone or something."* Ask: *What do a class, an orchestra, and a tour of a museum have in common?* Answer your question by saying: *They all need someone to conduct them.* Have students complete the Day 1 activities on page 123. You may want to do the first one as a group.

DAY 2

operate
(verb) To work or run. *The TV won't operate if it's not plugged in.*

Show students a common battery-powered device, such as a clock. Say: *This (device) operates on batteries. If I remove the batteries, it will not operate.* Explain that "operate" has the same meaning as "run" or "work." Then have students complete the Day 2 activities on page 123. You may want to do the first one as a group.

DAY 3

operate
(verb) To control the running of something. *I operate the TV when we use it in class.*

Ask: *What do a car, a computer, a pencil sharpener, and a CD player have in common?* Give students time to respond. Then answer your own question by saying: *They all need someone to operate them.* Discuss what a person does when he or she **operates** each of these things. Then have students complete the Day 3 activities on page 124. You may want to do the first one as a group.

DAY 4

process
(noun) A series of actions that make something. *We are learning the process of writing a good story.*

If you wish, use bread, peanut butter, and a knife to demonstrate this lesson. Say: *When you follow a process, you do several things to make something. One common process is to make a peanut butter sandwich. Can you tell me the process of making a peanut butter sandwich?* Make the sandwich exactly as the students tell you, or write the steps on the board. If the students miss any steps, prompt them to remember. Then say: *You explained the process of making a peanut butter sandwich.* Then have students complete the Day 4 activities on page 124. You may want to do the first one as a group.

DAY 5

Have students complete page 125. Call on students to read aloud their answers to the writing activity.

Daily Academic Vocabulary • EMC 2759 • © Evan-Moor Corp.

Name_____

Day 1 conduct

1. How would you complete these sentences? Say them aloud to a partner.

I would like to conduct an experiment on _____.

I think it would be fun to conduct a tour of _____.

2. Which of these things could someone *conduct*? Circle your answers.

a. a dictionary

c. a survey

b. an investigation

d. dinner

3. In which sentence could *conduct* take the place of "lead"? Circle your answer.

a. Clues sometimes <u>lead</u> you to the wrong conclusion.

b. Mr. Holland will <u>lead</u> a tour of the public gardens.

c. All three paths <u>lead</u> to the same place.

d. The mayor's float will <u>lead</u> the parade.

Day 2 operate

1. How would you complete this sentence? Say it aloud to a partner.

_____ is something in my home that uses batteries to operate.

2. Name three things that *operate* on electricity.

a. _____

b. _____

c. _____

3. Which of these things *operate* by wind power? Circle your answers.

a. a flashlight

c. a sailboat

b. a kite

d. a microwave

What do you operate on?

Day 3 operate

1. How would you complete this sentence? Say it aloud to a partner.

When I grow up, I would like to operate a _____.

2. Which of these things can you *operate* now? Circle your answers.

    a. a bike   c. a school bus

    b. a helicopter   d. a computer

3. In which of these sentences could *operate* <u>not</u> take the place of "run"? Circle your answer.

    a. The Andersons <u>run</u> a farm stand on Route 32.

    b. Peter's older brother will <u>run</u> in a 5K race.

    c. You need to be careful when you <u>run</u> any kind of machine.

    d. The school buses do not <u>run</u> on weekends.

Day 4 process

1. How would you complete this sentence? Say it aloud to a partner.

In school, I have learned the process of _____.

2. Which phrase best completes this sentence? Circle your answer.

The scientific process _____.

    a. makes science

    b. tells you facts about the solar system

    c. uses specific actions to answer a scientific question

    d. uses guessing to answer a scientific question

3. Which *process* would you use to decide which movie to watch with your friends? Circle your answer.

    a. voting process   c. writing process

    b. number process   d. scientific process

Day 5 **conduct • operate • process**

Fill in the bubble next to the correct answer.

1. If you *conduct* a meeting, you _____.

Ⓐ do all the talking

Ⓑ listen and say nothing

Ⓒ lead it and direct it

Ⓓ invite your friends to come

2. Which sentence uses the word *operate* correctly?

Ⓕ The refrigerator operates very quietly.

Ⓖ This road operates alongside the river.

Ⓗ The idea operated through her mind.

Ⓙ The story will operate in all the newspapers.

3. You press a button to *operate* _____.

Ⓐ a suitcase

Ⓑ a picnic basket

Ⓒ a phone

Ⓓ a drawer

4. Which number *process* is used to solve this problem: $3 \times 5 =$ _____?

Ⓕ addition

Ⓖ division

Ⓗ multiplication

Ⓙ subtraction

Writing Imagine you had a chance to *conduct* a tour. Where would you like to *conduct* it? Tell about the place and why you would like to show others around it. Use the word *conduct* in your writing.

_____

_____

_____

WEEK 30

view • approach

Use the transparency for week 30 and the suggestions on page 6 to introduce the words for each day.

DAY 1

view
(noun) What you see from where you are. *The house has a view of the lake.*

(verb) To see or look at. *Our class viewed the jellyfish exhibit the day it opened at the aquarium.*

Ask students to look out a classroom window and tell what they see (use the door if no window). Say: *You just described the view from our window. You told me what you view when you look out.* Then ask: *Have you ever heard someone talk about a nice view? Where could you go to see a nice view?* Encourage students to use **view** in their responses. Then have students complete the Day 1 activities on page 127. You may want to do the first one as a group.

DAY 2

approach
(verb) To move nearer. *The children will approach the dog carefully.*

Ask a student to come to your desk. Then say: *(Student's name) just approached my desk. When you approach something, you move closer to it.* Ask: *In what situations do things or people approach, or move closer to, something else?* (e.g., cars **approach** an intersection; runners **approach** the finish line) Say: *Things can move closer in time, as well as space. What do you look forward to approaching?* (e.g., the weekend; holidays) Then have students complete the Day 2 activities on page 127. You may want to do the first one as a group.

DAY 3

approach
(verb) To begin or prepare to work on something. *How will you approach the word problem?*

Say: *Approach can also mean to begin something. I approach a new unit we will study by thinking and reading about it. How do you approach writing a story? How do you begin? How would you approach your homework?* Then have students complete the Day 3 activities on page 128. You may want to do the first one as a group.

DAY 4

approach
(noun) A way of dealing with something. *When we didn't understand the new math concept, our teacher tried a different approach.*

Pose a problem for the students. For example, ask: *How would you help a first-grade student who was having trouble with addition?* Have several students share their ideas. Comment on each idea using the word **approach**. Then ask: *If someone tells you to try a new approach to something, what does that mean?* Then have students complete the Day 4 activities on page 128. You may want to do the first one as a group.

DAY 5

Have students complete page 129. Call on students to read aloud their answers to the writing activity.

Daily
Academic
Vocabulary

Day 1 view

1. How would you complete these sentences? Say them aloud to a partner.

My favorite view is the one from _____.

I would like to view _____.

2. Which words might describe the *view* from a mountaintop? Circle your answers.

a. beautiful   c. ordinary

b. small   d. breathtaking

3. Where would you go to *view* these things? Draw lines to show your answers.

a. waves crashing on the beach   an art museum

b. paintings and drawings   a city park

c. dinosaur bones   the seashore

d. people jogging and skating   a natural history museum

Day 2 approach

1. How would you complete this sentence? Say it aloud to a partner.

I always slow down when I approach _____.

2. Which sentence uses the word *approach* correctly? Circle your answer.

a. Our campsite approached a clearing in the woods.
b. We woke up as soon as the sun approached in the sky.
c. We saw a deer and a fawn approach the clearing.
d. They ran away as soon as they approached us nearby.

3. Which of these things are you glad to see *approach*? Circle your answers.

a. your birthday   c. a big test
b. a visit to the doctor for shots d. summer vacation

Day 3 approach

1. How would you complete this sentence? Say it aloud to a partner.

I always approach my schoolwork by _____.

2. Which phrases best complete this sentence? Circle your answers.

The best way to approach a problem is _____.

   a. to think it cannot be solved

   b. to believe it can be solved

   c. to look at all sides of the problem

   d. to understand just a small part of the problem

3. What are two things you do when you *approach* writing a story?

   a. _____

   b. _____

Day 4 approach

1. How would you complete this sentence? Say it aloud to a partner.

One approach to memorizing a poem is _____.

2. Which phrase best completes this sentence? Circle your answer.

If you have a new approach to a problem, you _____.

   a. have a problem no one else has ever had

   b. think of a different way to deal with it

   c. do what everyone else does

   d. do what you always do

3. Which one do you think is the best *approach* to studying for a spelling test? Circle your answer.

   a. Study right before the test.   c. Quickly read the words.

   b. Watch TV while you study.   d. Read and write the words every day.

Daily Academic Vocabulary

| **Day 5** | **view • approach** |

Fill in the bubble next to the correct answer.

1. In which sentence is the word *view* <u>not</u> used correctly?

Ⓐ Everyone was eager to view the new movie.

Ⓑ The hotel room had a view of the park.

Ⓒ We could not view if the bike had a flat tire.

Ⓓ From the plane, we had a great view of the city at night.

2. If you are *approaching* your ninth birthday, _____.

Ⓕ you are already nine

Ⓖ you are worrying about it

Ⓗ your birthday is getting closer

Ⓙ your birthday already happened

3. If you are *approaching* a problem, you are _____.

Ⓐ figuring out how to deal with it

Ⓑ getting closer to it

Ⓒ trying to get away from it

Ⓓ pretending there is no problem

4. You might try a different *approach*, if _____.

Ⓕ your old methods always work

Ⓖ you don't like what you have to do

Ⓗ you don't know what you want to do

Ⓙ you didn't have success the first time

Hiccup!
Hiccup!
Hiccup!

Writing Explain your favorite *approach* to dealing with hiccups. Be sure to use the word *approach* in your writing.

_____

_____

_____

content • contents • feature

Use the transparency for week 31 and the suggestions on page 6 to introduce the words for each day.

DAY 1

content
(noun) The information that is in a book or other written work. *The content of the magazine is all about nature.*

Hold up one of the students' textbooks. Ask: *What is the content of this book? What information do we find in this book?* Hold up another textbook and ask the same questions. Help students conclude that the **content** is the information a book contains. Then have the students complete the Day 1 activities on page 131. You may want to do the first one as a group.

DAY 2

contents
(noun) The things found inside something, such as a container. *Because the label came off the can, nobody knows its contents.*

Without students' knowledge, fill an opaque bag with small objects from the classroom. (e.g., pencils; markers; crayons) Show the bag to students and have them guess the **contents**. Say: *The contents of this bag are a mystery. Guess the contents of the bag.* After guesses, empty the **contents** onto a table. Say: *I have just emptied the contents of the bag on the table. Let's see if your guesses about the contents were correct.* Then have students complete the Day 2 activities on page 131. You may want to do the first one as a group.

DAY 3

feature
(noun) An important part or quality of something. *Clues are always an important feature of a mystery story.*

Name some fables that are familiar to all the students. (e.g., "The Tortoise and the Hare"; "The Lion and the Mouse") Say: *A feature is the important part or quality of something.* Ask: *What feature is common to all these stories?* (e.g., they teach lessons; they are all fables) Then say: *Stories aren't the only things that have features. What would you say is a feature of our school? What is an important part of it?* (e.g., friendly spirit; great teachers; artwork in the hall) Then have students complete the Day 3 activities on page 132. You may want to do the first one as a group.

DAY 4

feature
(verb) To give special attention to. *The magazine featured the story about the rainforest.*

Show students copies of children's publications, such as *Ranger Rick.* Read the titles of the articles in the magazine. Then show the cover. Ask: *Which article is featured on the cover?* Say: *In magazines, the cover picture relates to the article that is featured, or given special attention.* Then have students complete the Day 4 activities on page 132. You may wish to do the first one as a group.

DAY 5

Have students complete page 133. Call on students to read aloud their answers to the writing activity.

Daily Academic Vocabulary

Day 1 content

1. How would you complete this sentence? Say it aloud to a partner.

I would choose a library book that had content about _____.

2. What kind of textbook would have this *content*? Circle your answer.

• *How Things Move* • *How Plants Make Food* • *Rocks and Minerals*

a. science
b. language arts
c. social studies
d. health

3. Which of these things would <u>not</u> be part of the *content* of a reading book? Circle your answer.

a. stories
b. math problems
c. poems
d. nonfiction articles

Day 2 contents

1. How would you complete this sentence? Say it aloud to a partner.

The contents of my bedroom include _____.

2. What do you think are the *contents* of this bag? Circle your answer.

a. zipper, straps, student
b. dog, cat, hamster
c. books, homework, pencils
d. school, home, library

3. What do you think are the *contents* of this basket? Circle your answer.

a. clothes hangers
b. books
c. washing machine
d. dirty clothes

Day 3 feature

1. How would you complete this sentence? Say it aloud to a partner.

My favorite feature of our community is _____.

2. List two *features* that make a big city different from a small town.

a. _____

b. _____

3. Which one is <u>not</u> a *feature* of a map? Circle your answer.

a. shows you where things are

b. a key or legend

c. a computer

d. helps you get from one place to another

Day 4 feature

1. How would you complete this sentence? Say it aloud to a partner.

If I wrote a play, I would feature a part for _____.

2. Which phrase best completes this sentence? Circle your answer.

A school newspaper would feature _____.

a. articles written by scientists

b. stories and articles by students

c. state and national news

d. weather reports from around the world

3. In which sentence is the word *feature* used correctly? Circle your answer.

a. The science fair will feature our class's science project.

b. An article about Mars features the magazine.

c. Mars is featured by its red glow in the night sky.

d. Mars is commonly feature "The Red Planet."

Daily Academic Vocabulary

Day 5 | content • contents • feature

Fill in the bubble next to the correct answer.

1. Which of these things does <u>not</u> have *content*?

Ⓐ a Web site

Ⓑ a book

Ⓒ a blank notebook

Ⓓ a magazine

2. Which of these would <u>not</u> be among the *contents* of the art supply closet?

Ⓕ pairs of scissors

Ⓖ paintbrushes

Ⓗ a pair of rubber boots

Ⓙ colored construction paper

3. In which sentence could you use the word *feature* to fill in the blank?

Ⓐ The children's room is the best _____ of our library.

Ⓑ A library card is a _____ for checking out books.

Ⓒ There is a _____ if you return a book late.

Ⓓ The _____ tells you where to find a book.

4. If an actor is *featured* on a TV show, she _____.

Ⓕ has a very small part

Ⓖ is seen but doesn't speak

Ⓗ appears in the first 3 minutes

Ⓙ has a large part

Writing What is one *feature* of your favorite book? Why do you like it so much? Be sure to use the word *feature* in your writing.

_____

_____

_____

purpose • object • objective

Use the transparency for week 32 and the suggestions on page 6 to introduce the words for each day.

DAY 1

purpose
(noun) The reason something exists; its use. *The **purpose** of this button is to turn on the computer.*

Direct attention to the classroom clock. Ask: *Why do we have a clock on the wall? What is the **purpose** of the clock?* Repeat this with other classroom objects—the pencil sharpener, the wastebasket, the board—each time asking students to define the object's **purpose**. Then have students complete the Day 1 activities on page 135. You may want to do the first one as a group.

DAY 2

purpose
(noun) The reason why something is done. *The **purpose** of the meeting was to plan the school fair.*

Say: *When I ask you to read to find out a certain thing, that is your **purpose** for reading.* Ask: *If I ask you to read a story to learn about Africa, what is your **purpose** in reading that story?* (to learn about Africa) Then say: *Authors write stories for many reasons. We call those reasons the author's **purpose**. Authors might want to tell you something that really happened, or they might want to make you laugh. What other **purposes** could an author have?* Then have students complete the Day 2 activities on page 135. You may want to do the first one as a group.

DAY 3

object
(noun) Something that can be seen and felt, but is not alive. *Marcie spotted a shiny **object** in the sand.*

Show students a pencil, an eraser, and a ruler. Say: *These are **objects** found in a classroom.* Name other localities (e.g., a kitchen; a gym; a library) and have students name **objects** that would be found in each place. Then have students complete the Day 3 activities on page 136. You may want to do the first one as a group.

DAY 4

objective
(noun) Something that one tries to achieve; purpose. *The **objective** of our project is to learn about sharks.*

Write the word **objective** on the board. Circle the word "object" within it. Say: *You've probably heard the word "object" used as "the object of the game." **Objective** is similar because it is something you try to achieve. My **objective** in school is to teach you what you need to know this year.* Ask: *What is an **objective** you have at school?* If you write lesson **objectives** on the board, be sure to integrate them into your discussion of **objective**. Then have students complete the Day 4 activities on page 136. You may want to do the first one as a group.

DAY 5

Have students complete page 137. Call on students to read aloud their answers to the writing activity.

Name_____

Day 1 purpose

1. How would you complete this sentence? Say it aloud to a partner.

For me, the purpose of a phone is to _____.

2. Connect each object with its *purpose*. Draw lines to show your answers.

a. a light switch   to lock and unlock a door

b. a key   to turn lights on and off

c. a water faucet   to write something down

d. a pencil   to control the flow of water

3. Which phrase best completes this sentence? Circle your answer.

The purpose of an umbrella is to _____.

a. match your raincoat
b. bring bad luck if you open it indoors
c. prevent you from getting wet in the rain
d. lend it to a friend

Day 2 purpose

1. How would you complete this sentence? Say it aloud to a partner.

My purpose for writing a book report is _____.

2. Which sentence correctly uses the word *purpose*? Circle your answer.

a. Oversleeping was my purpose for being late.
b. My purpose for calling is to ask about our homework.
c. Studying hard is the purpose I did well on the test.
d. He had no purpose to lie about what happened.

3. What do you think is your teacher's *purpose* for giving you homework?

_____

_____

Day 3 object

1. How would you complete this sentence? Say it aloud to a partner.

My favorite object in this room is _____ because _____.

2. List a different *object* that you might use in each of these subjects.

a. science _____

b. social studies _____

c. art _____

d. math _____

3. Which of the following things is <u>not</u> an *object*? Circle your answer.

a. a water bottle   c. a hamster

b. a cage   d. a running wheel

Day 4 objective

1. How would you complete this sentence? Say it aloud to a partner.

My objective in school is _____.

2. Which phrase best completes this sentence? Circle your answer.

The objective of the student art sale is _____.

a. next Saturday and Sunday   c. in the school gym

b. to raise money for more art supplies   d. my favorite school day

**3. If your *objective* is to grow a sweet potato vine, you need _____.
Circle your answer.**

a. a sweet potato, a jar, and water   c. to bake a sweet potato

b. a fork, salt, and butter   d. to like sweet potatoes

Daily Academic Vocabulary

Day 5 purpose • object • objective

Fill in the bubble next to the correct answer.

1. The *purpose* of a doorknob is _____.

Ⓐ to decorate the door

Ⓑ to open a door

Ⓒ for you to hang your jacket on it

Ⓓ to be a shiny object

2. Which of the following is <u>not</u> a *purpose* for going to the library?

Ⓕ to mail a letter

Ⓖ to find a book about dolphins

Ⓗ to return a book you borrowed

Ⓙ to check out books to read for fun

3. Which sentence could <u>not</u> be completed with the word *object*?

Ⓐ Rob found the _____ he was looking for.

Ⓑ Which _____ did you find on the ground?

Ⓒ The parakeet stared at its _____ in the mirror.

Ⓓ Thalia chose the _____ she liked best.

4. Which sentence uses the word *objective* correctly?

Ⓕ The woman objective to the store's prices.

Ⓖ Our objective was to get to the airport on time.

Ⓗ If no one has objective, we can start tomorrow.

Ⓙ Ben slipped the objective into his pocket.

Writing Tell about an *objective* you might have if you went on a hike. Be sure to use the word *objective* in your writing.

_____

_____

_____

judge • judgment • prove disprove • proof

Use the transparency for week 33 and the suggestions on page 6 to introduce the words for each day.

DAY 1

judge
(verb) To form an opinion about something. *They bought the car they **judged** to be the safest.*

judgment
(noun) An opinion about someone or something. *He tries not to make a **judgment** about people he's just met.*

Show students three books. Point to one of the books and say: *I think this book is the best of the three.* Then say: *I just **judged** the books and shared my opinion about which one is the best. I made a **judgment** about the books.* Ask: *When do you **judge** things or make **judgments**? When do you form opinions about something? Have you made **judgments** about movies? Have you **judged** TV shows?* Then have the students complete the Day 1 activities on page 139. You may want to do the first one as a group.

DAY 2

judgment
(noun) The ability to make wise choices. *We trusted Mom's **judgment** in all important matters.*

To help students think about this meaning of **judgment**, say: *When a person can make good choices, we say that person has good **judgment**. What words would describe a person with good **judgment**?* (e.g., wise; intelligent) *With poor **judgment**?* (e.g., foolish; careless) Then have students complete the Day 2 activities on page 139. You may want to do the first one as a group.

DAY 3

prove
(verb) To show that something is true. *Can you **prove** that pencil is yours?*

disprove
(verb) To show that something is false. *Beth **disproved** the idea that boys run faster than girls by winning the race.*

Write this math problem on the board: "6 + 5 = 11." Say: *I can **prove** this.* Count out 6 counters. Then count 5 counters. Put the two groups together and count the total number: 11. Say: *By counting, I **proved** that 6 + 5 = 11.* Then write this problem on the board: "13 − 8 = 6." Say: *I can **disprove** this.* Count out 13 counters. Remove 8. Then count the ones remaining. Ask: *How did I **disprove** 13 − 8 = 6?* Then have students complete the Day 3 activities on page 140. You may want to do the first one as a group.

DAY 4

proof
(noun) Facts or evidence that something is true. *Emma's grades were **proof** she worked hard in school.*

Explain that **proof** is related to "prove." Say: *When you provide the **proof**, you prove that something is true.* Ask: *What kind of **proof** would show that a book belongs to you?* (e.g., your name written in the book) *What kind of **proof** would show that you had read a story?* (e.g., being able to retell what happened) Then have students complete the Day 4 activities on page 140.

DAY 5

Have students complete page 141. Call on students to read aloud their answers to the writing activity.

Name_____

Day 1 **judge • judgment**

1. How would you complete these sentences? Say them aloud to a partner.

I try not to judge people until _____.

Before I make a judgment about a book, I will _____.

2. An old saying is, "Don't *judge* a book by its cover." What does this mean? Circle your answer.

    a. Don't choose a book for a judge unless it has a nice cover.

    b. Don't weigh a book without including its cover.

    c. Don't form an opinion based only on what you can first see.

    d. Don't write a book report if all you've read is the cover.

3. Which of these situations require making a *judgment*? Circle your answers.

    a. selecting a new pair of shoes

    b. deciding who can be trusted with a secret

    c. eating lunch

    d. waiting for the school bus

Day 2 **judgment**

1. How would you complete this sentence? Say it aloud to a partner.

I think I have good judgment when it comes to _____.

2. In which sentence is the word *judgment* used correctly? Circle your answer.

    a. The teacher had a calm and caring judgment.

    b. Elias showed good judgment when he chose his team.

    c. Loyalty is a common judgment of a dog.

    d. Celia made a strong judgment for going to the water park.

3. Which of these actions would you say shows good *judgment*? Circle your answer.

    a. staying up late on a school night

    b. riding your bike on a crowded sidewalk

    c. petting a strange dog

    d. choosing healthy snacks

Name _____

Day 3 **prove • disprove**

1. How would you complete these sentences? Say them aloud to a partner.

I can prove _____ by _____.

I can disprove that I am only five years old by _____.

2. Circle the statements you could *prove*. Underline the statements you could *disprove*.

a. Wood floats.

b. A feather falls faster than a rock.

c. Plants need water and light.

d. Yellow and red make blue.

3. Which of these sentences do <u>not</u> use *prove* or *disprove* correctly? Circle your answers.

a. Mother disproves when we yell in the house.

b. The experiment proves that oil floats on water.

c. I set out to disprove her claim that she was the fastest runner.

d. The fingerprints are prove that someone touched the wet paint.

Day 4 **proof**

1. How would you complete this sentence? Say it aloud to a partner.

The work I do in school is proof that I _____.

2. What would be *proof* for each of the statements at the left? Draw lines to show your answers.

a. Deer ate the flowers.   measuring the sides

b. The triangle has three equal sides.   dried mud on his shoes

c. David stepped in a mud puddle.   a stuffy nose and coughing

d. Amelia has a cold.   deer tracks in the flower bed

3. Which ones show *proof* that you finished your homework? Circle your answers.

a. Your teacher checked it.

b. You put your books away.

c. A parent made sure you did it.

d. You decided to watch TV.

Name_____

Day 5 | judge • judgment
prove • disprove • proof

Fill in the bubble next to the correct answer.

1. If you *judge* something, then you _____.

Ⓐ decide that it's bad

Ⓑ enter it in a contest

Ⓒ form an opinion about it

Ⓓ choose it over other things

2. In which sentence could *judgment* take the place of the underlined word?

Ⓕ We trust Dad's opinion when it comes to food.

Ⓖ Our book club made the decision to meet on Thursday.

Ⓗ The successful science fair was the result of careful planning.

Ⓙ Tomika used her imagination to picture a beautiful white sand beach.

3. Which of the following is something you cannot *prove* or *disprove*?

Ⓐ an answer in math

Ⓑ a science fact

Ⓒ an opinion

Ⓓ that something happened

> What **proof** do you have that I drank the milk?

4. The empty milk carton is *proof* that _____.

Ⓕ milk is good for your bones

Ⓖ everyone should drink milk

Ⓗ milk should come in bottles

Ⓙ someone drank the last of the milk

Writing   What is something you can *prove?* How can you *prove* it?
Be sure to use the word *prove* in your writing.

_____

_____

_____

assist • assistance
cooperate • cooperation

Use the transparency for week 34 and the suggestions on page 6 to introduce the words for each day.

DAY 1

assist
(verb) To help or give aid to someone. *Jenna* **assisted** *the teacher by putting away the art supplies.*

Ask a student: *Will you* **assist** *me in drawing a house on the board?* Take turns drawing parts of a house on the board. Ask the student's opinion about what to include or how to draw the house. Then say: *Thank you for* **assisting** *me. You helped me draw this house. I am glad you could* **assist** *me.* Then have students complete the Day 1 activities on page 143. You may want to do the first one as a group.

DAY 2

assistance
(noun) Help or aid. *Everyone offered* **assistance** *to clean up the room.*

Show students a deck of cards. Say: *I'm going to do a card trick, but I need some* **assistance**. Have a volunteer select a card. Try to guess the card the student selected. Make several random guesses. (The routine is meant to be funny.) Then say: *Well, I need to work on that trick, but I thank (student's name) for his (or her)* **assistance**. Ask: *When have you needed* **assistance** *in something?* Then have students complete the Day 2 activities on page 143. You may want to do the first one as a group.

DAY 3

cooperate
(verb) To work together. *The students should* **cooperate** *during their group project.*

Say: *When you work with someone, you* **cooperate**. *Right now, we are* **cooperating** *on learning the meaning of the word* **cooperate**. Ask: *With whom do you* **cooperate** *in school? At home? What do you* **cooperate** *on?* Then have students complete the Day 3 activities on page 144. You may want to do the first one as a group.

DAY 4

cooperation
(noun) The act of working together. *The* **cooperation** *of the team members helped them win the game.*

Say: *When you cooperate, you show* **cooperation**. ***Cooperation*** *happens when you cooperate, or work together, with someone. Many jobs, activities, and sports require* **cooperation** *for success. Think about my job as a teacher. If we did not have* **cooperation** *in the classroom, then you would not learn, and I would not have successfully done my job.* Then ask: *What other jobs do you think require* **cooperation**? *What activities? What sports?* Encourage students to use the word **cooperation** in their responses. Then have students complete the Day 4 activities on page 144. You may want to do the first one as a group.

DAY 5

Have students complete page 145. Call on students to read aloud their answers to the writing activity.

Name_____

Daily Academic Vocabulary

Day 1 assist

1. How would you complete this sentence? Say it aloud to a partner.

I am happy to assist anyone who _____.

2. Which of these jobs could you *assist* with at home? Circle your answers.

a. preparing meals

b. washing the dishes

c. feeding a pet

d. washing the clothes

3. Which phrase best completes this sentence? Circle your answer.

We can assist the teacher by _____.

a. talking all at once

b. listening and following directions

c. being mean to our classmates

d. not doing our work

Day 2 assistance

1. How would you complete this sentence? Say it aloud to a partner.

I need an adult's assistance in order to _____.

2. In which sentence is the word *assistance* <u>not</u> used correctly? Circle your answer.

a. We needed assistance when we got a flat tire.

b. Moira did her homework without assistance from anyone.

c. The assistance crowd cheered for the team.

d. I needed assistance when I was learning to ride my bike.

3. What can you do with *assistance* and without *assistance*? Write some examples.

<u>What I Can Do with Assistance</u>   <u>What I Can Do without Assistance</u>

a. _____   a. _____

b. _____   b. _____

c. _____   c. _____

Day 3 cooperate

1. How would you complete this sentence? Say it aloud to a partner.

I often cooperate with _____ to _____.

2. Which people on the left need to *cooperate* with the people on the right? Draw lines to show your answers.

a. the school principal   other people in government

b. the president of a country   other members of the team

c. the captain of a basketball team   the director of a play

d. actors   teachers

3. In which sentence is the word *cooperate* used correctly? Circle your answer.

a. Kylie knew she could cooperate on her own.

b. Justin and Colin knew they must cooperate to finish on time.

c. The teacher told the group she was happy with their cooperate.

d. Dan cooperated when he took the pen away from Selene.

Day 4 cooperation

1. How would you complete this sentence? Say it aloud to a partner.

It takes cooperation to _____.

2. Which phrase correctly describes *cooperation*? Circle your answer.

a. working together   c. performing surgery

b. making others do things   d. doing everything yourself

3. Which sentence correctly describes an act of *cooperation*? Circle your answer.

a. Shana watched her brother make his bed.

b. Mr. Clark told the students how to complete the project.

c. Marie searched the Internet for information.

d. Alex helped Adrian finish his chores so they could go to the park.

Name _____

Day 5 | **assist • assistance**
cooperate • cooperation

Fill in the bubble next to the correct answer.

1. If you *assist* someone, you _____.

Ⓐ invite the person to your home

Ⓑ help the person do something

Ⓒ try to make the person agree with you

Ⓓ try to keep out of the person's way

2. Which of these words could <u>not</u> take the place of *assistance* in a sentence?

Ⓕ help

Ⓖ aid

Ⓗ bother

Ⓙ support

3. Which word does <u>not</u> complete this sentence correctly?

When you cooperate, you _____.

Ⓐ help

Ⓑ aid

Ⓒ support

Ⓓ change

Cooperation is always important!

4. In which sentence could *cooperation* be used to fill in the blank?

Ⓕ The teacher insisted on _____ among the students.

Ⓖ The project required that _____ be the result of one student.

Ⓗ The team _____ to win the game.

Ⓙ Do the _____ homework on your own.

Writing Describe the last time you *cooperated* with someone on a school project. Be sure to use one of this week's words in your writing.

_____

_____

_____

expect • predict
prediction • predictable

Use the transparency for week 35 and the suggestions on page 6 to introduce the words for each day.

DAY 1	**expect** *(verb)* To think that an event or action is likely to happen. *We expect Grandma to visit next week.*	Ask: *What do you expect we will do in school tomorrow?* As students suggest activities, ask them to tell the reason why they **expect** this. (e.g., we do it every day; you already told us this would happen) Then have students complete the Day 1 activities on page 147. You may want to do the first one as a group.
DAY 2	**predict** *(verb)* To tell in advance what you think will happen in the future. *I predict that it will rain tomorrow.*	Show students a wet sponge. Ask: *What you do predict will happen if we leave this wet sponge on the table overnight?* Explore with students the prior knowledge they used to **predict** that the sponge will be dry by the next day. Ask: *Why do you predict the sponge will be dry?* Say: *When you predict, you use what you already know to tell what you think will happen.* Then have students complete the Day 2 activities on page 147. You may want to do the first one as a group.
DAY 3	**prediction** *(noun)* An event that is told before it happens. *It is my prediction that our team will win.*	Show students the sponge you left out overnight. Say: *Yesterday it was your prediction that this sponge would be dry today. Is that what happened?* Point out that when they made their **prediction**, they said what would happen before it actually did happen. Invite students to tell about other **predictions** they have made. Encourage them by mentioning sports, grades, books, and movies. Then have students complete the Day 3 activities on page 148.
DAY 4	**predictable** *(adj.)* Happening in a way or at a time in which you could have expected. *Recess is predictable because it happens at the same time every day.*	Remind students that at the beginning of the week you talked about what they expected to happen in school the next day. Say: *You can expect certain things to happen at school because we follow a routine. What we do is predictable.* Invite students to suggest other things that are **predictable**. (e.g., bedtime; mealtimes; when you get up) Then have students complete the Day 4 activities on page 148. You may want to do the first one as a group.
DAY 5		Have students complete page 149. Call on students to read aloud their answers to the writing activity.

Name_____

Day 1 | expect

1. How would you complete this sentence? Say it aloud to a partner.

I expect a funny movie to _____.

2. Study this pattern. If the pattern continued, what shape would you *expect* to come next? Circle your answer.

○ ☆ ◇ ♡ ◇ ☆ ○ ☆ ◇ ♡ ◇ ☆ ○ ☆ ◇ ♡ ◇ ☆ ○ ☆ ◇

a. ○   b. ☆   c. ◇   d. ♡

3. In which sentence is *expect* <u>not</u> used correctly? Circle your answer.

a. Good teachers expect all their students to learn.

b. We expect to get our book reports back today.

c. Someone should expect the bike to be sure it's safe.

d. We expect to leave on vacation in six weeks.

Day 2 | predict

1. How would you complete this sentence? Say it aloud to a partner.

I predict that this afternoon at 5 o'clock, I will _____.

2. *Predict* something that will happen on each of these days. Write what you *predict*.

a. tomorrow _____

b. Saturday _____

c. Monday _____

3. Which phrase best completes this sentence? Circle your answer.

When you predict while reading, you _____.

a. think about what will happen when you stop reading

b. try to figure out what will happen next in the story

c. try to decide if you like the story

d. think about who else has read this book

Day 3 prediction

1. How would you complete this sentence? Say it aloud to a partner.

My prediction for this summer is that _____.

2. Which one of these statements is a *prediction*? Circle your answer.

   a. The library always has a summer reading program.

   b. Every year there is a different topic.

   c. This year's topic is "Adventuring with Books."

   d. I think we're going to read some exciting books.

3. In which sentence is the word *prediction* used correctly? Circle your answer.

   a. It is my prediction that you will like this story very much.

   b. It takes prediction to be able to write a good story.

   c. You need to put the characters in an interesting prediction.

   d. There needs to be exciting events and a happy prediction.

Day 4 predictable

1. How would you complete this sentence? Say it aloud to a partner.

I like things to be predictable because _____.

2. List three things that are *predictable* in your life.

   a. _____

   b. _____

   c. _____

3. Which phrase best completes this sentence? Circle your answer.

If someone is predictable, _____.

   a. you never know what she will do

   b. she always surprises you

   c. you always know what to expect

   d. she can tell you what the weather will be tomorrow

Name_____

Daily Academic Vocabulary

| Day 5 | expect • predict
prediction • predictable |

Fill in the bubble next to the correct answer.

1. If you expect something to happen, you _____.

Ⓐ are afraid that it won't happen

Ⓑ don't know that it will happen

Ⓒ have reason to believe that it will happen

Ⓓ have no idea when it will happen

2. Which sentence uses the word *predict* correctly?

Ⓕ Dora likes to predict she is a famous person.

Ⓖ Can you predict how many beans are in the jar?

Ⓗ Greg's little brother likes to predict he's a dog.

Ⓙ Can you predict how the story would end?

3. When you make a *prediction*, you _____.

Ⓐ figure out the answer to a problem

Ⓑ put events in the order in which they happen

Ⓒ tell what's going to happen before it does

Ⓓ don't understand what's going on

*I **predict** that you will do well on this test!*

4. If a TV show is *predictable*, _____.

Ⓕ there are lots of surprises

Ⓖ you know what will happen next

Ⓗ it is probably about the past

Ⓙ you can't wait to see it again

Writing   Make a *prediction* about something that will take place at school in the next few weeks. Be sure to use the word *prediction* in your writing.

_____

_____

_____

approach

assist

assistance

conduct

content

contents

cooperate

cooperation

disprove

expect

feature

judge

judgment

label

object

objective

operate

predict

predictable

prediction

process

proof

prove

purpose

term

view

Days 1–4

Each day's activity is a cloze paragraph that students complete with words or forms of words that they have learned in weeks 28–35. Before students begin, pronounce each word in the box on the student page, have students repeat each word, and then review each word's meaning(s). **Other ways to review the words:**

- Start a sentence containing one of the words and have students finish the sentence orally. For example:

  *I know how to **operate** a…*
  *I **predict** that tomorrow we will…*

- Provide students with a definition and ask them to supply the word that fits it.

- Ask questions that require students to know the meaning of each word. For example:

  *What is the **object** of the game of checkers?*
  *What is the **purpose** of a light switch?*

- Have students use each word in a sentence.

Day 5

Start by reviewing the words in the crossword activity for Day 5. Write the words on the board and have students repeat them after you. Provide a sentence for one of the words. Ask students to think of their own sentence and share it with a partner. Call on several students to share their sentences. Follow the same procedure for the remaining words. Then have students complete the crossword activity.

Extension Ideas

Use any of the following activities to help integrate the vocabulary words into other content areas:

- Have students explain how they would **approach** finding out what animals live in the Arctic National Park and Preserve.

- Introduce or revisit the writing **process**. Assign a piece of writing and take students through each step. At the end, **conduct** a discussion with students about how the writing **process** helps them be better writers.

- Have students explain how they would **prove** or **disprove** this statement: Oil and water do not mix. Allow students to **conduct** their experiments.

- Assign students partners. Give each pair a blank map and a student atlas of South America. Have them **label** each country and capital. Allow them to ask for **assistance** from you if necessary.

Daily Academic Vocabulary

approach	cooperation	judge	predict
conduct	expect	judgment	prove
content	feature	objective	

Day 1

Fill in the blanks with words from the word box.

You can't _____ a book by its cover, but the cover

can help you choose a book. The cover gives you hints about the

book's _____. Covers usually _____ a brief

summary of the book. It tells you what you can _____.

Then you can use your _____ to decide if the book is one

you will enjoy.

Day 2

Fill in the blanks with words from the word box.

Inquiry is the way that scientists _____ answering

scientific questions. First, they decide what they want to find out and

set their goal or _____. Next, they plan experiments and

_____ what the experiments will _____ or

disprove. Then, they _____ the experiments and study

the results. It often takes the _____ of many

scientists to discover new things.

| assist | contents | labels | predictions | term |
| assistance | features | objects | purpose | view |

Day 3

Fill in the blanks with words from the word box.

"Buddy Reading" is a _____ for reading with a

partner. A person who reads well reads with someone who is learning

to read. The better reader gives _____ in figuring

out words and their meanings. The buddies talk about the different

_____ of the story and make _____ about

what will happen. The _____ of Buddy Reading is to help

someone learn to read better.

Day 4

Fill in the blanks with words from the word box.

Mr. Cross is making a science lab in our classroom. He asked

Serena to help and _____ him. Mr. Cross is putting all

the lab supplies in clear glass containers. That will make it easy to

_____ the _____ of the containers. Serena

is helping by making _____ for the jars and for other

_____ used in the lab.

Name_____

Day 5

Crossword Challenge

For each clue, write one of the words from the
word box to complete the puzzle.

| assist | disprove | operate | process |
| cooperate | object | predictable | proof |

Down

1. to work together
3. happening in the way you expect
4. a series of actions that make
   something
5. facts that show something is true

Across

2. to work or run
6. to show that something is false
7. to help
8. something that can be seen

Answer Key

Week 1

Day 1
2. c
3. a. the solar system—science
   b. subtraction—math
   c. our country's history—social studies
   d. nouns and verbs—writing

Day 2
2. c
3. Answers will vary.

Day 3
2. a, c
3. b

Day 4
2. b
3. Answers will vary.

Day 5
1. A   2. H   3. D   4. H

Week 2

Day 1
2. a, d
3. b, c

Day 2
2. b, c
3. c

Day 3
2. c
3. b

Day 4
2. b
3. c

Day 5
1. B   2. F   3. C   4. J

Week 3

Day 1
2. b, d
3. a, c

Day 2
2. c
3. Answers will vary.

Day 3
2. b
3. Answers will vary.

Day 4
2. a, c
3. d

Day 5
1. B   2. G   3. B   4. H

Week 4

Day 1
2. a, d
3. b, d

Day 2
2. c
3. c, d

Day 3
2. b
3. a. Tuesday—Tues.
   b. Avenue—Ave.
   c. February—Feb.
   d. Ohio—OH

Day 4
2. b
3. a, d

Day 5
1. C   2. H   3. A   4. H

Week 5

Day 1
2. b
3. b

Day 2
2. c
3. a. noticeable—able to be noticed or seen
   b. familiar—well-known
   c. author—the writer of a story, book, article, or play
   d. possess—to have or own something

Day 3
2. a
3. d

Day 4
2. b, d
3. c, d

Day 5
1. C   2. J   3. A   4. J

Week 6

Day 1
2. b
3. c

Day 2
2. a, d
3. b

Day 3
2. d
3. a

Day 4
2. d
3. b, c

Day 5
1. B   2. F   3. D   4. G

Week 7

Day 1
2. a, c
3. c

Day 2
2. c
3. b

Day 3
2. a. to get on the bus—form a line
   b. to talk about books—form a book club
   c. to play a basketball game—form two teams
   d. take turns driving—form a car pool
3. c

Day 4
2. a, d
3. b, d

Day 5
1. A   2. J   3. B   4. G

Week 8

Day 1
2. a
3. a. a fairy tale—with "and they lived happily ever after"
   b. a tic-tac-toe game—with one player getting three in a row
   c. a concert—with the audience clapping
   d. a day—with the sun going down

Day 2
2. c
3. d

Daily Academic Vocabulary • EMC 2759 • © Evan-Moor Corp.

Day 3
2. a. cat hair on someone's clothes—The person has a cat.
   b. people walking with open umbrellas—It is raining outside.
   c. someone yawns—The person needs a nap.
   d. the dog runs to the door and barks—Someone is at the door.
3. b
Day 4
2. b
3. d
Day 5
1. D 2. G 3. B 4. H

Week 9 Review

Day 1
unusual, increase, subject, definitely
Day 2
revisions, edited, brief, decreased
Day 3
forms, defined, conclude, definition, pause
Day 4
abbreviation, abbreviate, usual, definite
Day 5
1. brief   4. conclude
2. revise   5. increase
3. form   6. regular
code answer: lemurs can be found

Week 10

Day 1
2. a, c
3. b, d
Day 2
2. a
3. d
Day 3
2. c
3. a. celebrate someone's birthday—arrange a birthday party
   b. see lions and tigers—arrange a trip to the zoo

c. have shorter hair—arrange to get a haircut
   d. be sure your pet is healthy—arrange a trip to the vet
Day 4
2. a
3. a, d
Day 5
1. C 2. F 3. B 4. J

Week 11

Day 1
2. d
3. c
Day 2
2. a. The Big Plant—"Jack and the Beanstalk"
   b. Emily and the Enchanted Frog—"The Frog Prince"
   c. When I Was Young in the Mountains—the author's own life
   d. How Lion Became King of the Animals—an African folk tale
3. a, d
Day 3
2. d
3. Answers will vary.
Day 4
2. c
3. c
Day 5
1. D 2. G 3. C 4. H

Week 12

Day 1
2. a. animal lovers—being mean to animals
   b. people who love trees—cutting down forests
   c. people who clean up parks and beaches—litter
   d. people who love to read—the library closing
3. Answers will vary.
Day 2
2. Answers will vary.
3. c
Day 3
2. a, d
3. c

Day 4
2. a. Anna and Ted walked on opposite—sides of the street.
   b. The library is on the opposite corner from—City Hall.
   c. Tia waved to Gus from the opposite—side of the room.
   d. The king and queen sat at opposite—ends of the table.
3. b
Day 5
1. C 2. G 3. D 4. J

Week 13

Day 1
2. b
3. d
Day 2
2. a
3. c
Day 3
2. d
3. c
Day 4
2. b
3. c
Day 5
1. C 2. J 3. B 4. G

Week 14

Day 1
2. a, b
3. c
Day 2
2. a, b
3. Answers will vary.
Day 3
2. c
3. c
Day 4
2. d
3. a, b
Day 5
1. C 2. G 3. A 4. J

Week 15

Day 1
2. c
3. d

Day 2
2. a
3. a. lots of scratching—The dog has fleas.
   b. putting suitcases in the car—The neighbors are going on a trip.
   c. buying a big bag of cat food—The woman has more than one cat.
   d. walking fast—The person is in a hurry.

Day 3
2. c, d
3. b

Day 4
2. a
3. c

Day 5
1. B   2. H   3. D   4. H

Week 16

Day 1
2. a, c
3. Answers will vary.

Day 2
2. c
3. Answers will vary.

Day 3
2. b
3. b, d

Day 4
2. c
3. c

Day 5
1. C   2. G   3. A   4. H

Week 17

Day 1
2. b
3. a

Day 2
2. a, b
3. b

Day 3
2. c
3. a, d

Day 4
2. c
3. b

Day 5
1. A   2. H   3. C   4. F

Week 18 Review

Day 1
basic, arrangement, suggest, occur

Day 2
basics, total, sum, exactly

Day 3
summarize, events, occurrence, summary

Day 4
arrange, modeled, copies, opposite, generalization

Day 5
Across
1. basis
5. suggestion
8. oppose

Down
2. arrangements
3. claim
4. base
6. general
7. exact

Week 19

Day 1
2. a, d
3. b

Day 2
2. d
3. Answers will vary.

Day 3
2. c, d
3. d

Day 4
2. a, c
3. b

Day 5
1. A   2. H   3. C   4. H

Week 20

Day 1
2. a. A good skater might attempt—to skate backward.
   b. Someone who likes to write might attempt—to write a book.
   c. A good swimmer might attempt—to swim the length of the pool.
   d. A fast runner might attempt—to win a race.
3. Answers will vary.

Day 2
2. c
3. b, d

Day 3
2. c
3. fail, fail, fail

Day 4
2. a, d
3. Answers will vary.

Day 5
1. D   2. G   3. C   4. J

Week 21

Day 1
2. a, d
3. Are we supposed to answer the question on the board?

Day 2
2. d
3. b

Day 3
2. c
3. b

Day 4
2. a
3. c

Day 5
1. C   2. H   3. B   4. F

Week 22

Day 1
2. a. The ocean contains—different kinds of sea animals.
   b. A dictionary contains—words and their meanings.
   c. A magazine contains—articles and pictures.
   d. An airplane contains—people traveling somewhere.
3. Answers will vary.

Day 2
2. d
3. c

Day 3
2. a. papier-mâché—strips of paper, paste
   b. a birthday party—cake, friends, presents

c. a circus—animals, acrobats, clowns

d. a friendship—common interests, caring, shared times

3. a

Day 4

2. a. names of states—Maine, Florida, Texas, Oregon

b. kinds of trees—oak, maple, pine, redwood

c. parts of a book—title, table of contents, index, glossary

d. bodies of water—oceans, rivers, lakes, ponds

3. d

Day 5

1. D   2. H   3. A   4. J

Week 23

Day 1

2. b

3. a. A whistle produces— a loud blast of sound.

b. A dairy produces—milk, cheese, and ice cream.

c. A campfire produces— heat and light.

d. A fan produces— a cool breeze.

Day 2

2. d

3. c

Day 3

2. b

3. b

Day 4

2. c

3. a

Day 5

1. C   2. J   3. C   4. G

Week 24

Day 1

2. a, d

3. d

Day 2

2. c

3. c

Day 3

2. a. You eat too much food.— You get a stomachache.

b. You get sick.—You stay home from school.

c. A mosquito bites your arm. —You get an itchy bump.

d. You wear shoes that don't fit.—You get a blister on your foot.

3. a, d

Day 4

2. d

3. c

Day 5

1. C   2. G   3. C   4. J

Week 25

Day 1

2. a, d

3. d

Day 2

2. c

3. b, c

Day 3

2. b

3. a, c

Day 4

2. a. A pilot—has control over a plane.

b. A firefighter—takes control over fires.

c. A coach—has control over the players.

d. A leader—takes control of a group.

3. Answers will vary.

Day 5

1. B   2. H   3. D   4. H

Week 26

Day 1

2. c

3. Answers will vary.

Day 2

2. a, d

3. d

Day 3

2. a, c

3. Answers will vary.

Day 4

2. a, c

3. d

Day 5

1. C   2. F   3. B   4. J

Week 27 Review

Day 1

consider, produced, effective, control

Day 2

memorize, recite, decide, consisted, attempted, fail

Day 3

products, questions, contains, cause, Failure

Day 4

recount, inquiry, recall, include

Day 5

1. decision   4. inquire
2. attempt   5. effect
3. memorize   6. inquiry

code answer: perspiration

Week 28

Day 1

2. b

3. c

Day 2

2. a, d

3. c

Day 3

2.

3. a, b

Day 4

2. c

3. a, d

Day 5

1. B   2. G   3. A   4. H

Week 29

Day 1

2. b, c

3. b

Day 2

2. Answers will vary.

3. b, c

Day 3

2. a, d

3. b

Day 4
2. c
3. a

Day 5
1. C   2. F   3. C   4. H

Week 30

Day 1
2. a, d
3. a. waves crashing on the beach—the seashore
   b. paintings and drawings—an art museum
   c. dinosaur bones—a natural history museum
   d. people jogging and skating—a city park

Day 2
2. c
3. a, d

Day 3
2. b, c
3. Answers will vary.

Day 4
2. b
3. d

Day 5
1. C   2. H   3. A   4. J

Week 31

Day 1
2. a
3. b

Day 2
2. c
3. d

Day 3
2. Answers will vary.
3. c

Day 4
2. b
3. a

Day 5
1. C   2. H   3. A   4. J

Week 32

Day 1
2. a. a light switch—to turn lights on and off
   b. a key—to lock and unlock a door
   c. a water faucet—to control the flow of water

   d. a pencil—to write something down
3. c

Day 2
2. b
3. Answers will vary.

Day 3
2. Answers will vary.
3. c

Day 4
2. b
3. a

Day 5
1. B   2. F   3. C   4. G

Week 33

Day 1
2. c
3. a, b

Day 2
2. b
3. d

Day 3
2. circle: a, c; underline: b, d
3. a, d

Day 4
2. a. Deer ate the flowers.—deer tracks in the flower bed
   b. The triangle has three equal sides.—measuring the sides
   c. David stepped in a mud puddle.—dried mud on his shoes
   d. Amelia has a cold.—a stuffy nose and coughing
3. a, c

Day 5
1. C   2. F   3. C   4. J

Week 34

Day 1
2. Answers will vary.
3. b

Day 2
2. c
3. Answers will vary.

Day 3
2. a. the school principal—teachers
   b. the president of a country—other people in government

   c. the captain of a basketball team—other members of the team
   d. actors—the director of a play
3. b

Day 4
2. a
3. d

Day 5
1. B   2. H   3. D   4. F

Week 35

Day 1
2. d
3. c

Day 2
2. Answers will vary.
3. b

Day 3
2. d
3. a

Day 4
2. Answers will vary.
3. c

Day 5
1. C   2. J   3. C   4. G

Review Week 36

Day 1
judge, content, feature, expect, judgment

Day 2
approach, objective, predict, prove, conduct, cooperation

Day 3
term, assistance, features, predictions, purpose

Day 4
assist, view, contents, labels, objects

Day 5
Down
1. cooperate
3. predictable
4. process
5. proof

Across
2. operate
6. disprove
7. assist
8. object

Index